# ARTISTRY OF
# PEGGY KARR GLASS

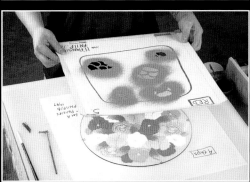

**PEGGY KARR**

Schiffer Publishing Ltd ®

4880 Lower Valley Road, Atglen, PA 19310 USA

## DEDICATION

This book is dedicated to my husband and business partner Tim Seitz. His unwavering enthusiasm, hard work and support has helped make Peggy Karr Glass what it is today.

# ACKNOWLEDGMENTS

I would like to personally thank Lynda Portelli, Yolanda Fundora, Tara Elms, Jennifer Zausmer, Derek Seitz, and Tim Seitz for their tremendous help with this book. There were thousands of transparencies to go through, digital files to find, tons of data to organize, text to edit, and art work to create. Their generous hard work, and support have helped to make this book a reality.

Library of Congress Cataloging-in-Publication Data:

Karr, Peggy, 1953-
  Artistry of Peggy Karr Glass / by Peggy Karr.
    p. cm.
  ISBN 0-7643-2144-7 (hardcover)
1. Karr, Peggy, 1953- 2. Glass artists—United States—Biography. 3. Glass fusing—United States. 4. Peggy Karr Glass. I. Title.

NK5198.K37A2 2005
748'.092—dc22

2004017119

Designed by John P. Cheek
Type set in Futura Hv BT/Humanist 521 BT

ISBN: 0-7643-2144-7
Printed in China

Published by Schiffer Publishing Ltd.
4880 Lower Valley Road
Atglen, PA 19310
Phone: (610) 593-1777; Fax: (610) 593-2002
E-mail: Info@schifferbooks.com

For the largest selection of fine reference books on this and related subjects, please visit our web site at
**www.schifferbooks.com**
We are always looking for people to write books on new and related subjects. If you have an idea for a book please contact us at the above address.

This book may be purchased from the publisher.
Include $3.95 for shipping.
Please try your bookstore first.
You may write for a free catalog.

In Europe, Schiffer books are distributed by
Bushwood Books
6 Marksbury Ave.
Kew Gardens
Surrey TW9 4JF England
Phone: 44 (0) 20 8392-8585; Fax: 44 (0) 20 8392-9876
E-mail: info@bushwoodbooks.co.uk
Free postage in the U.K., Europe; air mail at cost.

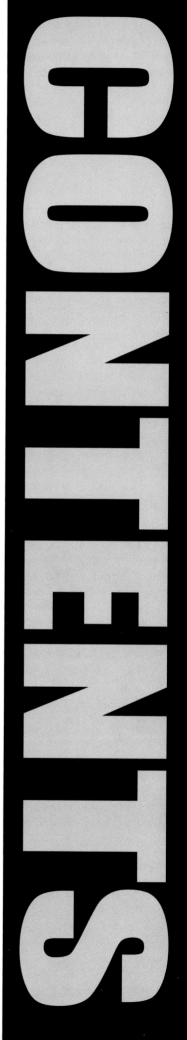

CONTENTS

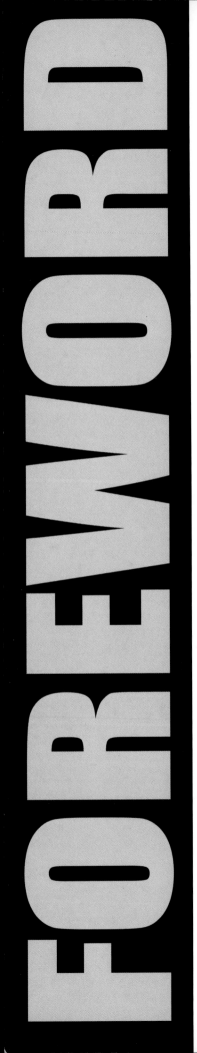

FOREWORD

Peggy Karr's tale is the kind that inspires, the kind of tale that excites, the kind of tale that elicits a smile and an admiring nod of the head.

I came to know Peggy three years ago, after following her and her company from a distance for some time. I have been a publisher and editor of *Tableware Today,* a trade magazine that covers all things tabletop, for the last ten years. I have interviewed hundreds of artisans. I am oftentimes humbled and awed by the sheer creative talent that has infused the tableware industry almost since the start of man. Contrary to popular belief, it is tableware that can probably be credited as the world's oldest profession. Cavemen, after all, were the most primitive artisans, fashioning utensils needed to prepare their food. Peggy's ancient fused glass technique was developed more than 4,000 years ago in Mesopotamia. Tableware design is rich in imagination, rich in ingenuity, and rich in innovation. Add Peggy Karr to the list of artists who have left an indelible mark thanks to an inimitable style and exceptional talent.

First things first, there is no doubt that Peggy's eponymous enterprise is a phenomenal success. Built from scratch to a multimillion-dollar business, Peggy has brought work to hundreds of people in northern New Jersey while creating the largest enameled fused glass facility in the world. More importantly, this self-professed hippie has been able to hold fast to ideals and philanthropic sensibilities sown early on, proving that good guys can indeed finish first. Peggy Karr's story is one of the more interesting I've told in twenty years of writing about the creative talents that percolate the tableware field.

Peggy supported an early ceramics muse by cleaning houses. For years, this Jersey girl figured the only way to feed her creative soul at night was by cleaning up after others during the day. That all changed in 1987 when she realized the only way to test her talents was to jump in full throttle, so armed with a dream and a kiln, which she hoisted three flights up to a makeshift studio in a church where she moonlit as a caretaker, Peggy started her experimentations with glass. It was love at first fuse. And an instant success; at her first trade show, Peggy, much to her surprise and delight, found herself with thousands of dollars in orders. No more cleaning houses from then on.

Peggy discovered a natural business acumen coupled with a healthy dose of common sense yielded a business growing at a feverish clip. It was so hot, Peggy's husband, Tim Seitz, recognized the potential and joined on. From the start, the ambitious and hardworking couple toiled without end, foregoing vacations, working weekends, literally pouring themselves into growing Peggy Karr Glass.

One of the things that impressed me most after visiting the Peggy Karr Glass factory in Randolph, New Jersey, is how much Peggy is loved and respected by her familial staff, and how hard she has worked to gain that trust. Peggy once said, "I work hard to know what's going on because when you're disconnected from your workers, you're disconnected from your company." This sentiment is precisely why the retail folks who buy her products love her, love her work, and love her company. It's why customers wait for hours to have Peggy sign their plates. It's why her dance card is always penciled in. It's a wonder Peggy ever finds time for her favorite pastime, riding her beloved horse Cromwell. It is exceedingly rare to find so much love between supplier and customer, but Peggy simply wouldn't know how to run her business any other way.

For years Peggy has found unique ways to leave her stamp: from cool corrugated pizza box packaging, to signing hundreds of plates a day at special events for avid collectors, to hiring family and friends when a cardinal rule of business is never hire family and friends.

Isn't it interesting that Peggy's designs are found in homes the world over, yet she has lived in the same area of northern New Jersey her entire life? Peggy could easily take her winnings and cash out on some tropical island, daiquiri in hand. But that's not Peggy. Peggy is a rare businesswoman who has managed to remain true to ideals and beliefs while running a phenomenally successful company that has her name on the door.

Amy Stavis
Editor/Publisher
*Tableware Today*
Holmdel, New Jersey

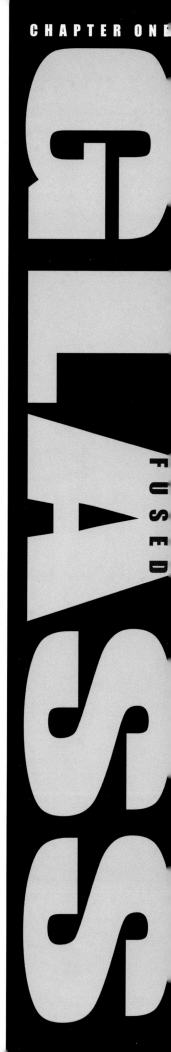

Peggy Karr with 11 inch plates on the back wall 2004.

I get a lot of questions about Peggy Karr Glass (PKG). How is it made? How did I get started? What is fused glass? And most importantly, the collectors want to know about all our old patterns. So, I decided it was time to write a book. I will do my best to answer these questions so everyone has a better understanding of Fused Glass in general and Peggy Karr Glass specifically. If I get too technical please forgive me, it is part of what I love about glass fusing; I am just as much a technician as I am an artist. I love exploring new possibilities and solving problems in a medium that is just now coming into its own.

Before I get into some of the details, this would be the time to talk about Fused Glass in general. Glass is a remarkable material. It is a solid but it also has the molecular qualities of a liquid. Its main ingredient is silica, better known as sand. When blended with other elements and melted at high temperatures in a furnace you get glass. When heated, it goes from a solid to a soft toffee-state. It will adhere to itself, bend and stretch like rubber, and finally flow like thick syrup. At any of these points rapid cooling will freeze the glass into the form that it has adopted.

There are three basic ways to work in glass. First is flat or cold glass. This method uses either clear or colored glass that has already been formed into sheets. It is then cut and assembled into architectural windows and doors. Stained Glass is found in this category as well as Sand Carving. Second is Blown or Hot Glass. This method takes molten glass and blows it into forms such as wine goblets, bottles, and vases, or rolls it into sheet glass for windows. This can be done either mechanically or by hand. The third is glass fusing or Warm Glass. This method takes cold sheet glass and reforms it with heat. This is how Peggy Karr Glass is made.

The term Warm Glass indicates the temperatures used to reform the glass. They are lower than those used to melt it for Hot Glass work. It is sometimes called bent, slumped, or kiln-fired, indicating the process it goes through in the kiln. As the temperature rises in the kiln, the glass first bends, keeping its hard edges and smooth finish. Next it will slump, becoming softer and taking on some of the texture of the mold. Pieces of glass will stick together but they will still have clear edges and appear separate. When the glass gets hotter it will fully fuse and will have melted together to form one piece of glass. If the temperature continues to rise, the glass will ultimately become a puddle in the bottom of the kiln.

As you can see, there are many ways to fire the glass. Most fused glass requires a mold to hold the glass in the kiln. One of the characteristics of Fused Glass is the surface texture you get from the mold.

Glass is extremely sticky and will permanently adhere itself to anything it touches, including the kiln itself. I have opened the kiln and found pieces stuck to the door. So, all the molds must be coated with something to keep the glass from adhering. At fusing temperatures glass will take on the pattern of anything it is touching, including the separator material, which is where the "characteristic texture" comes from. Your molds may be flat or bent; however, the slope can't be too steep or the glass will slide down the sides to the bottom. So, you can't make things like mugs or glasses with straight sides. Finally, there are millions of ways to decorate the glass. You can melt cut pieces of glass together, you can include other materials that can withstand the firing process, such as metal, or you can decorate with paints or enamels. I have chosen to focus on enamels that are applied dry with sifters and stencils and then encased between two pieces of clear glass.

The best way to understand how glass fusing got started is to go to the very beginning. Glass goes back millenniums; when formed by nature in volcanic eruptions it is known as obsidian or black glass. The Roman historian Pliny wrote that man first discovered glass making by accident about the year 5000 B.C. Phoenician sailors preparing a meal on a beach in Asia Minor couldn't find stones to place their cooking pots on so they set them on blocks of nitrum (soda and potash) carried by their ship as cargo. As the fires burned hotter, the sand and soda turned to molten glass. The authenticity of Pliny's account is now considered dubious but it contains an accurate recipe for producing glass: sand (silica), soda ash, and heat.

The first actual pieces of manmade glass date back to 2500 B.C. in Mesopotamia. Small glass vessels were formed by wrapping melted glass rods around a clay core. The clay was later removed after the glass had cooled. Glass beads and tiles were formed using the fusing method of melting glass together in a kiln. Glass blowing wasn't discovered until approximately 250 B.C. in Babylon. In the beginning glass making was a very carefully guarded secret and didn't become more wide spread until 100 A.D. From this point forward glass experiences tremendous growth and new discovery. There was the beautifully ornate glass of Murano, Italy, made around the thirteenth to fourteenth centuries. The Venetians called this clear thin glass Cristallo. Flat glass for windows was still rare during the seventeenth century and finally in the eighteenth and nineteenth centuries becomes more easily produced and windows become commonplace. Glass can now be made by machine. Near the turn of the twentieth century, Galle, Tiffany, and Steuben are founded. Between the 1930s and '40s "Carnival" and "Depression" glass are mass-produced. Glass is no longer available only to the rich.

That brings us to the current American studio glass movement of the 1950s and '60s. It is here where Glass Fusing is rediscovered after so many millenniums. Up until now factories with closely guarded secrets and expensive equipment have produced glass. Working in glass as a creative medium for independent artists has not been widely available. The American studio glass movement is started when Harvey Littleton and Edris Eckhardt begin to explore glass as a creative medium. They open the door to other artists who begin to experiment with different ways of working in glass. The Higgins, both Michael and Frances, start to produce fused glass in the late 1940s in their Chicago area studio. On the East Coast Maurice Heaton of Rockland County, New York, was starting to produce his bent enameled plates and lighting fixtures. Both of these artists can be credited with starting fused glass as we know it today. So no, I did not invent enameled glass nor did another recent artist discover it, as he claims, studying Ancient Egyptian artifacts. We all took classes or read books inspired by these two wonderful pioneers. As fused glass continues to grow in popularity I would like to think I was responsible for helping to make people more aware of the art form. I wasn't the first fuser, and I surely won't be the last, but I hope I will be thought of as a valuable contributor.

Michael and Frances Higgins, early 1970s. Photo from *Higgins Adventures in Glass*, a book for collectors covering the Higgins life and glassware by Schiffer Publishing. *Courtesy of Leslie Piña and Donald-Brian Johnson.*

I had to finish my Vortex panels for a glass conference in March and then started making bowls and dishes for my Spring sale. Due to an injury to my shoulder, this was so slow that some people left empty-handed. I will have a large choice as ever, in June, of my glass.

MAURICE HEATON
347 Old Mill Road
Valley Cottage, N.Y. 10989
(914) 268-2151

On March 26, 1987 County Executive John Grant presented Maurice Heaton with the First Annual County Executive's award for his "outstanding contributions to the arts and culture of Rockland County" as an individual visual artist.

Maurice Heaton, 1987.

## CHAPTER TWO

I am often asked how I got started in Fused Glass. When I think of all the twists and turns my life has taken I'm not really sure how or when Peggy Karr Glass began. There is a movie called *Sliding Doors,* staring Gwyneth Paltro, which begins one morning when she gets fired from her job. In one scenario she misses her train home and in another she doesn't. The movie follows the two scenarios and shows how her life is changed by this simple event and in some ways, how it stays the same. I sometimes wonder, if I had made other choices in the past, whether I would still have ended up in the same place.

I was born in 1953 in Arlington, New Jersey. My father was an Electrical Engineer for years but hated constantly having to find a new job once his project was finished, so one day he decided to become an antique clock dealer. I would sit on the basement stairs watching him repair the old clocks and was completely enthralled. I learned if you look very carefully at a problem, the solution is usually right in front of you. He taught me how to identify problems and test my solutions. My mother started out as just my mom but went back to social work when her children got older. She ultimately returned to school and became a Classical Freudian Analyst. She taught me how to look inward and understand myself; a gift I feel very lucky to have learned. Both of my parents are now retired and live nearby.

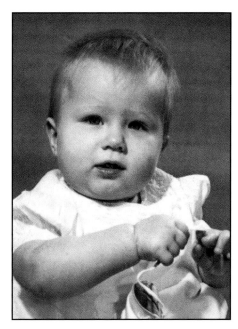

Peggy at six months, 1953.

Ruth and Alex Karr with Margaret Ann (Peggy) at four weeks, 1953.

Peggy and father Alex, 1954.

Peggy and brother Michael, 1956.

I have one brother, Michael, who is two years younger than me, and graduated Cum-Laude from Boston University with a degree in business. He has worked with me at PKG almost from the beginning. Michael spends his spare time buying and selling old paintings or competing in bicycle races. He has one daughter, Julianne, who has the Karr creative genes. I also have a sister, Ginny, who is six years younger than me. She has an associate's degree from Harcum and works a few days a week at the local veterinary clinic. She has three children, Allen, Rebecca, and Scott. Ginny used to work at PKG part time and her husband, George Haversang, currently works at PKG. Growing up we got along pretty well, except for the fights the three of us had over who got the window seats in the car.

I spent most of my growing up years in North Caldwell, New Jersey. As a kid I liked making things with my hands. I was endlessly coming up with some hair-brained scheme like designing a flying suit, which included detailed plans on how it was going to work. One year when I was about ten I decided I wanted to be a Kangaroo for Halloween. It made perfect sense because with a pouch I wouldn't have to carry my candy. My mother said if I wanted to be a kangaroo I had to make my own costume, so I did. It came out pretty well. The only problem was the tail, which I ended up having to carry! I also spent a lot of time building forts and my best effort was a tree house we built in an old cherry tree in the lot next to us. While searching for lumber I found a great board just the right size for part of the floor. Unfortunately for me, it was my father's drafting board. After no TV for a week, my dad helped me rebuild the tree house without his drafting board. I think even back then my need to create was strong.

Home in North Caldwell, New Jersey, 1961 - 1972.

Michael, Peggy, and Ginny, 1962.

Kangaroo Halloween Costume, 1964.

I have a lot of great memories growing up in our neighborhood. We all played together, boys and girls of varying ages, without the aid of our parents. We managed to choose teams, set up rules, and play ball together without a major incident except for when the ball ended up in Mr. Richards' garden; if caught, you were bound to get yelled at. I think I learned a lot about negotiating and working together as a team from those ball games.

I graduated from West Essex Regional High School in 1971. I would have to say I was a "hippie" and spent a lot of my time hanging around with friends. One of my favorite teachers was Mr. Hawthorne. He was my art teacher and turned me on to all kinds of projects that got me to use my creativity. I remember specifically a lion I made out of papier-mâché, which was quite realistic except for his mane made from a blue feather boa.

I think I still have him somewhere. I was not the best student and didn't get involved with after school activities. I always seemed too busy with my own projects at home. After high school I didn't go to college right away. Everyone else was going to school and seemed to know what they wanted. I didn't see the point in wasting my time taking courses I didn't care about. One of the things I learned in high school was that if I wasn't interested, trying

High School graduation photo, 1971.

to pay attention could be impossible. But, if I was interested, wild horses couldn't drag me away from a subject. My parents sometimes worried because if I were concentrating on something I would never even know they were there. I am still like that today. My husband has learned that he has got to get my full attention before asking me something important; otherwise I will have no recollection of what I agreed to. This sometimes works in my favor when I have to focus on a project. I am able to tune out the world completely and give all my attention to what I need to do.

After I graduated, I got a job working in the local mall and found a small apartment. I loved being out on my own. After a couple of years I decided to go back to school full time and attended William Paterson, a small local college. Not wanting to give up my apartment or independence, I worked nights as a waitress. I started out only taking classes that interested me. I majored in Art and Biology with minors in Ceramics, Physics, and Chemistry. My favorite professor in college was Mr. Schubert, who taught ceramics. He ignited my interest so much

that I took six courses with him. We were forever fighting over my desire to focus on production wheel throwing techniques and his desire to get me to work on more sculptural things. I finally got even with him when I started to make huge hand made free form vessels that took up all the space in the kiln. I actually use this technique today when I work on new molds for glass, so I guess he was right to get me to try other ways of working in clay. One of the things that gave me a lot of trouble was glaze formulas. It wasn't until I started working in glass that I finally understood why I was having so much trouble. If it wasn't for my experiences in ceramics, it may have taken me forever to figure out some of my glass problems. I often wonder how Mr. Schubert is doing and if he is still teaching at the college. I never actually graduated from William Paterson, as I couldn't seem to complete all of the "boring" course requirements. At this point in my life I realized I wasn't going to become a Veterinarian or a Geographical Oceanographer. I didn't have the patience or money to complete the Doctorate I would need to do the things that really interested me.

After I left college I discovered I still had a need to create. I bought a kiln and start to make pottery to sell at local craft fairs. I put all those production ceramic techniques from college to good use. The "Hippie" in me was very pleased. I didn't make enough money, so I fell into housework as the mainstay to make ends meet. It left me with enough energy to still pursue my artwork. Rick Dreyer came into my life and introduced me to Stained Glass. "WOW!" This is better than ceramics! I fell in love with all the wonderful color. We made a lot of things together and one of my favorite items was "Hermit Huts". We made these adorable glass terrariums that looked like houses and sold them at street fairs in Manhattan. You got to choose two free Land Hermit Crabs with every home. They were a huge success and I think Hermit Crabs became a popular pet store item shortly thereafter. Dennis Verbeck came into my life around 1975. I got him hooked on stained glass and together we combined antique dressers with new stained glass mirrors in the attached frames and sold them at flea markets. Dennis died very tragically in 1980 and it took me a long time to recover.

Peggy & Rick at a street fair in Manhattan selling stained glass Hermit Huts, 1976.

Peggy & Dennis at a flea market selling antique furniture with custom made stained glass mirrors, 1978.

I then went to live and work on a Standard Bred Race Horse Farm in Bedminster New Jersey. What a hoot! The owner was an eccentric millionaire. I started out grooming horses but ended up in the main house as a cook. The cook's job included preparing all of the meals and taking care of the owner's personal needs and I got the servant's quarters all to myself. It was quite an experience living in such opulence. The owner was supposed to go to Florida for the winter, which would leave the entire house to me with little demands on my time, but I had done such a good job of taking care of him he decided to stay up north. I left after only a year because the job ultimately left me with no time for myself.

Horses, by the way, are my other passion. Since I was six years old all I ever asked for was a horse and the first thing I bought with my hard-earned money in 1971 was a horse. April was a beautiful palomino quarter horse. I only kept her a few years but it fulfilled a long time dream. I can still close my eyes and remember the feeling of riding her bareback through the woods. It was difficult giving her up, but I had decided I wanted to go to college and I couldn't afford both.

Peggy & April bareback, 1972.

In 1981 I found this great opportunity to work for the Morristown Unitarian Fellowship of New Jersey. They owned a huge Georgian brick mansion that had been converted into a church. The building was three stories and had over forty rooms and the job included a small apartment on the third floor. The work was only part-time, mostly keeping an eye on everything and taking out the garbage. I went back to housework to fill in financially. I didn't want to be alone in this huge building, so I took on a roommate. Bill Forsyth moved in and we became best friends but not romantically involved. Try explaining that to boy friends back then. That was a very pivotal time for me. The Fellowship gave me space in the attic so I could have a place to do my artwork. Bill was a photographer so together we were each other's cheering squad. We had endless discussions on the merits of art and what we planned to do when we became famous. We consoled each other when our respective projects seemed to be floundering and I remember working into the wee hours of the morning trying one more thing when Bill would come up and keep me company. I got involved with some Fellowship Committees and ended up running part of their annual craft show. "AHA!" I learned about business, finance, and marketing. I also became part of a group called the Folk Project. The group was involved with folk music and ran a coffee house every Friday night at the local county park. I'm not the best singer so I helped out by operating the soundboard and setting microphones. I learned a lot about organization, management, and working together as a team. The pieces of my life were starting to fall together. I had the time; space, skills, and support I needed to succeed with my artwork.

Morristown Unitarian Fellowship, New Jersey, 1981-1989.

I was hopelessly hooked on glass and all of its marvelous colors. I started making custom stained glass windows and lamps in my attic studio. It was very tedious and time-consuming cutting hundreds of little pieces of glass, wrapping the outside edge with a "copper foil" tape, and later joining all the glass together by melting a special blend of metals along the copper foil called "soldering". The other method involved fitting the glass pieces together into a channel of metal called "leading". This was okay, but when I went to do the math I was only making five dollars an hour. I started to explore other ways of working in glass; there had to be a better way to assemble all of those little pieces of color. I saw an interesting piece of glass in an antique shop and started a quest to find out how it was made. I located a book written by Harriet Anderson called *Kiln-fired Glass*. Maurice Heaton had been her teacher. "WOO HOO!" I dug out my old kiln from my ceramic days and I was off at a full gallop.

My original intent was to make this fabulous lamp by fusing all the little pieces of glass together. It never really looked as good as it did in my imagination so I finally gave up on the lamp idea but, what I had learned I started to apply to other projects. It took me a few years of endless experiments before I produced anything saleable.

Most of the information on fusing was vague and scarce but, that never slowed me down. I couldn't wait to get home to try something new. After a full day of cleaning, I would go upstairs and plan another experiment only to open the kiln and find another disaster.

I only had a simple ceramic kiln that operated manually back then. The firing cycle would take five to six hours to complete. If I turned the kiln on at eight at night it wouldn't finish until long after midnight so I would set my alarm and have to go up and watch the kiln until it reached the right temperature, and then turn it off manually. I had to sit on a wooden stool because if I got too comfortable I would fall back to sleep, over fire the kiln, and loose all my work. That never seemed to stop me.

Most of my friends thought I was crazy. "WHY DON'T YOU JUST GIVE UP?" I couldn't. One experiment led to the next experiment, which led to the next. I think this is how you become an addict. I took classes wherever I could find them. I took one class in Connecticut where I spent more time answering the teacher's questions than learning anything new. It was a two-weekend seminar, so I just skipped the second weekend. The teacher called me and wanted to know when I could come up and finish the class. This was when I realized I knew more than I thought I did. The other good thing that came from that weekend was meeting Phyllis Martin, who later introduced me to Rick Knopf. Both were budding glass artists and we spent a lot of time together sharing ideas and trying to hone our fusing skills. I began to focus on refining my techniques and applying them to specific projects. All the possibilities were great but I still had to apply them to something.

Custom Stained Glass Lamp, 20", 1983.

Custom Stained Glass Table, 46" x 28", 1984.

Combination Fused Glass and Stained Glass Screen, 1985.

Detail from combination Glass and Stained Glass Screen, 1985.

Early Fused Glass Plate, 14 inches, 1984.

Early Fused Glass Platter, 20 inches, photographed in attic studio, 1986.

Fused Glass wall sculpture, 26" x 18", 1985.

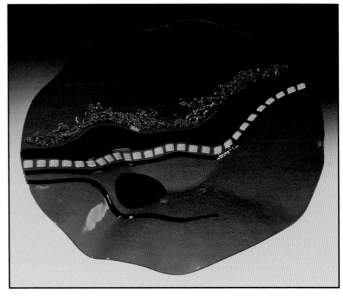

Early Fused Glass Platter, green, 20 inches, 1986.

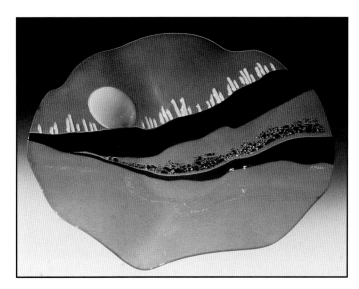

Early Fused Glass Platter, orange, 20 inches, 1986.

Early Fused Glass Platter, 16 inches, 1987.

My early pieces were very geometric and contemporary. I started out cutting and melting only glass. I now had the freedom to be more creative without the constraints of having to lead or foil the glass together as in stained glass. I sometimes combined fused pieces with leaded panels creating floor screens, coffee tables, and windows. I also did a series of large free form sculptural platters. I joined an artist co-op called "Art Showcase" where we collectively ran a gallery and I again reflected on the fact that I didn't make enough to survive without the cleaning. Well, you don't have to hit me over the head twice. I was exhibiting at a craft fair and I watched the woman next to me sell hundreds of ceramic pots decorated with cows and pigs. I quickly gave up the idea of becoming a famous "Artist" and applied my craft to making the first checkerboard cow. Here was something on which I could build a commercial business.

I started to work with enamels so I could get a lot more detail. It was impossible to cut little pieces of glass that small or intricate, plus I had to find a way to decorate the glass more efficiently. With enamels I still had all the great colors and I could make a plate in less than half the time. I remember cutting my first stencil and enameling that first plate. When I opened the kiln the next day I was in heaven. It worked! Little did I know what was in store for me in the future. Peggy Karr Glass was officially born in 1987. "AT LAST!" I finally got to quit cleaning.

I met my husband, Tim Seitz, a divorced father of two, at the Fellowship where he had been a member for years. We dated for a year, fell in love, and were married in 1989. Here is where you may ask, "what about children?" I was thirty-six when we got married. I had already started Peggy Karr Glass, so my life was pretty busy. I'm not sure if bad timing had children eluding me or I had been eluding them. Either way, Tim already had two nearly grown children, Derek and Kirsten, so we decided against having children ourselves. However, I have had an endless array of dogs, cats, and horses if that counts. I currently own a Caviler King Charles Spaniel named Miss Molly. I bring her to work every day and she has everyone wrapped around her little paw. She is my first purebred dog after many pound puppies and she knows she's royalty. I rediscovered horses again in 1995. Riding is the only time I really stop thinking about PKG. I own a wonderful, accomplished dressage horse named Cromwell, who knows a lot more about dressage than I do. He's been trying to teach me the finer points of riding.

Peggy & Molly, 2002.

Peggy Karr Glass truly is a "family affair." My brother Michael has been with me since almost the beginning, first as a glasscutter and currently as chief financial officer. My sister, Ginny, helped out in customer service in the beginning before she left to raise her family. Her husband, George, started in 1993 as plant Manager and was pivotal in developing our kilns. His cousin, Ed, runs our shipping department along with his wife, Donna. My nephew, Allen, has also spent summers working in the shipping department with Ed.

My husband, Tim, joined the company with trepidation in 1992 as Marketing Manager. He is a graduate of Westminster Choir College and is a fabulous tenor. He has performed across the country under people like Leonard Bernstein and Dave Brubeck. Later he took up business and started "The Musik Store." His passion has always been marketing and he was the driving force in the growth of PKG. We meshed together perfectly. I was able to focus more on the creative parts of the business while he took over the marketing.

We worried that it might affect our marriage but that was over ten years ago, so I guess we've withstood the test of time. Since we work together all day we have found that separate leisure activities are a must. Tim is an avid golfer while I choose to ride horses. Tim's daughter, Kirsten, worked in the shipping department for a while before she went off to graduate school in California to get her Masters in Statistics. Tim's son, Derek, joined the company in 2003 and was appointed Chief Operating Officer in 2004. I don't know how we got everything done without him. Derek's wife, Allyson, ran our factory outlet store and worked in customer service before she left to raise their family.

One of the rules of business is, "Never hire family or friends." It's not true. I have hired both and have found it to be extremely rewarding. I did, however, lose one very good friend in the beginning because we couldn't agree on how to run the business. In an attempt to salvage our relationship I asked her to leave, which, I'm sorry to say, completely ended our friendship. I have been lucky to have a lot of great friends join the company including Patsy, Suzanne, Shannon, and Yolanda, to name a few. I have also hired husbands, wives, children, and relatives and it all seems to have worked out to everyone's benefit. Peggy Karr Glass has been the collaborative effort of many talented people without whom I couldn't have gotten it all done. I am already looking at nieces, nephews, and grandchildren as the new generation for the future.

As I look back over my life I am overwhelmed with a sense of accomplishment. I got to realize my dreams. I got to do what I love for a living. It was a huge amount of work in the beginning, working twelve-hour days sometimes seven days a week … but it was worth every minute.

Peggy & Tim, 1990.

Peggy & Tim's wedding photo. L-R: Tim's son Derek; mother Evelyn; daughter Kirsten; Tim & Peggy; sister Ginny; Ginny's son Allen & husband George; Peggy's father Alex; sister-in-law Joanne & daughter Julianne; Mother Ruth and brother Michael, 1989.

## CHAPTER THREE

## Morristown Unitarian Fellowship
## 1987

My first studio was in the attic of the Morristown Unitarian Fellowship in Morristown, New Jersey. I had been living there as the caretaker since 1981. The Fellowship was a large Georgian brick mansion built in 1925 and the Unitarians let me use the attic with the conditions that I clean it up and leave some storage space for them. It was filled with years of old projects and forgotten furniture. Armed with a broom and some garbage cans, I carved out my first studio around 1983. The attic was large and had a trap door in the center with stairs that led to the flat part of the roof. On cool summer nights I would take a lawn chair up there while the kiln was firing and count shooting stars.

Peggy Karr in warehouse with shipping crates. 2004.

Peggy decorating in her attic studio, 1987.

Peggy's first custom kiln in her Fellowship studio, 1987.

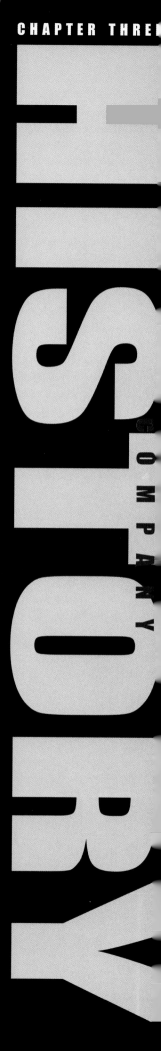

HISTORY COMPANY

I officially started Peggy Karr Glass in February of 1987. After years of countless experiments refining my fusing skills I finally had something I felt I could market successfully. From the beginning I decided I didn't want to sell retail. After years of trying to sell my other creations, I realized I wasn't very good at it. If I tried too hard I felt desperate, but when I gave up too easily I felt defeated. If someone gave me a lot of compliments I would feel self conscious and awkward, so for me it always seemed like a no win situation. Plus, the thought of making the plates all week and then having to sell them at craft fairs all weekend was the worst. That would also mean I had to work seven days a week and I was trying to find a way to work less, not more. The other down side of selling at craft fairs was that some were lucrative and some were not.

I wanted a more secure and regular income so I decided to try wholesale. Initially I had to create samples of all my plates, but then I only had to go to a few wholesale shows and take orders. The other plus was that I knew how much work I had to produce based on my orders. I could then plan how many plates I needed to make each week, take Sunday off, and know where my next dollar was coming from. The down side was selling my plates for only half of what the store would. I carefully looked at my production costs, sharpened my pencil, and came up with my first little wholesale catalog. The pros of selling wholesale outweighed the cons.

The most interesting part of doing trade shows was meeting all the people. Most shows lasted for five days and they happened twice a year. By the end of the third day things start to slow down and you become best friends with the other exhibitors around you. I got to talk business with others who really understood and I also got to meet and spend time with my customers. It was much easier for me to develop relationships with my stores than to make a one-time sale at a craft fair. I am much better with people I know, I feel more relaxed and able to share ideas. Over the years I would get to know many of these people very well. They gave me a lot of good feedback, which helped improve Peggy Karr Glass

Our Current booth, built in 1998.

In February of 1987 I attended my first wholesale trade show with trepidation. I invested most of my savings to pay for a booth at The Wendy Rosen's Buyers Market and later The New York Gift Show. The Buyers Market is a wholesale show open to only American craft artisans, which is now held twice a year in Philadelphia. It is filled with the most incredible handmade American crafts. Wendy Rosen started the show in 1985 in response to the growing demand for quality American made crafts. Retail Craft Shops were popping up everywhere and Wendy saw the need to get buyers and sellers together and the show has been a success ever since. The New York International Gift Fair is also a wholesale show operated by George Little Management. They are old pros at running wholesale trade shows. They have been doing them so long I sometimes think they invented them. They run them like a tight ship. It's hard to believe that all those boxes and crates that contain our booths and samples get to the right place and are transformed into this fabulous show. It's gigantic, with thousands of booths that fill the Jacob Javits Convention Center. There is everything you can imagine, from candles to expensive vases selling for hundreds of dollars.

I was afraid that no one would even notice me. But to my complete amazement I took thousands of dollars in orders at my first shows. Not only that, but then the stores started to place reorders. The first designs were a checkerboard motif with animals and vegetables. They were a perfect blend of country charm with a little hint of contemporary polish. They were available in round plates and bowls in several different sizes.

I clearly remember cutting those first stencils with a handheld X-acto™ knife. I was so careful not to waste anything that I saved each little scrap of cardboard. Today we go through pallets of stencil board a year. I had to hire my first two employees, Mary Kay and Carol, and we had a blast making plates in my attic studio. There were three flights of stairs, so all the glass had to be carried up and all the plates had to be

First booth at The Buyer's Market in 1987.

carried down. I had never been a boss before, but they were kind to me and I was a fast learner.

I had my first official "second" sale at the Fellowship. One of my friends was visiting and saw a large box of loose plates by the stairs. She asked what they were. I said they were rejects and I was going to throw them out. She was completely horrified! So, I said if she wanted to rescue them she could take whatever she wanted. She felt she couldn't just take them. She wanted to give me something, so we settled on five dollars each. She reflected that many of her friends would love to go through the box of plates as well. We planned a "Plate Party" and it was lots of fun, sort of like a Tupperware Party for fused glass. Everyone went home happy. They all said they had other friends who would love to come the next time I collected a box of rejects so the list kept growing. In the end we had a mailing list with thousands of names and we would have the sales three times a year. They even grew too large for our factory and we had to rent a local banquet hall to accommodate everyone. It was wild. People would line up an hour before we opened. Then there was the mad dash to find the best plates. By Sunday my husband, Tim, would be having these unbelievable specials to get rid of plates we didn't want to pack up after the sale and people would go crazy following him around waiting for his next announcement. We opened our outlet store in late 2001 and had our last Second Sale. People were sad to see them go but our little factory store is open three days a week and we still have all kinds of specials.

Lining up for the 2nd Sale at a local banquet hall, 1998.

Inside view of 2nd Sale at a local banquet hall, 1998.

## LATTELL ROAD, EAST HANOVER, NEW JERSEY 1988 – 1989

The Fellowship studio was too small and impractical to run a business. In 1988 I moved into a 2,000 square foot commercial space in East Hanover, New Jersey. I signed a two-year lease and was scared to death. How was I ever going to afford all this? The space, however, was marvelous. No more stairs and we even had a small loading dock. The building was in an industrial park just off a main highway with two offices in the front and open space in the back. We left one office for paperwork and designing and turned the larger one into the decorating room. The open area in the back was for the kilns, glass-cutting, and shipping. With the help of friends I renovated and built everything from scratch. I didn't have enough money to buy fancy metal shelves or worktables, but it didn't matter, I was in heaven. This was the studio of my dreams. Amazingly, we would outgrow the space before my lease was up and have to move to larger quarters again.

Left to Right—Liz, Gus (the dog), Peggy, Margy, Patsy, Mary Kay, Chris, Pat and Carol

First location in East Hanover. Employee group photograph, 1988.

At Lattell Road there were eight women, including myself. I remember one rainy day we got most of our work done early so we all went to the movies together on my nickel. We made a great team with everyone doing everything. We all decorated the plates, loaded the kilns, packed the orders, and cut the glass. When they asked if they could try designing a plate I thought why not. I discovered how talented they all were. I added some of their designs to my little catalog and it worked to everyone's advantage. Almost all of our designers today have come from the decorating department and have been with me for years. It takes a lot of talent to design for fused glass. It may look simple but there are lots of technical details and rules to follow. Experience from decorating makes it easier to understand the process.

My brother, Michael, began to help me part time, starting out by cutting glass. Then in 1993 when I needed someone to take over the finances and the scheduling of production, he would join the company full time. Michael was perfect; he held a degree in business from Boston University as well as having had experience in small business.

We were at Latell Road just long enough for me to learn what kind of space I would need when I had to move the business to larger quarters.

## HORSE HILL ROAD, CEDAR KNOLLS, NEW JERSEY 1989 – 1999

I was sad to see East Hanover go, but now I had 6, 000 square feet to play with. A computer company owned the 24, 000 sq. ft. building and we occupied the rear. Again the caravan of pick-up trucks and vans hauled all of my equipment to the new location. Again we built more wooden shelves and tables. This was the perfect place for us because as we continued to grow the computer company continued to shrink. They began to replace their large mainframe computers with small PC's so we were able to rent more space just when we needed it without having to move again. We were able to really settle in and get down to business.

Second location in Cedar Knolls. Employee group photograph 1996.

It's funny the things you remember. The building backed up to a small patch of woods and there was this little Plover, a bird who makes its nest on the ground, who tried to raise a family on the back edge of our parking lot. She was forever going into a tirade when you parked too close to her brood. She returned every spring without fail, unwilling to give up her little patch of ground.

Business was booming. We added a few more trade shows and I had to devise a calendar system to keep track of all our orders. We were still doing everything on paper and if we weren't careful we could sell more plates than

we could make. One of my secrets to success was listening to my customers. The stores wanted to know when they would get their order, so we always tried to deliver when we said we would. That meant the store was happy and would keep ordering.

My friend Suzanne joined the company in 1990. She stepped into customer service and started to get things done. It was no small feat to gets us organized and computerized. None of us were computer literate and trying to find computer programs was a nightmare. We got talked into having someone write a custom program for us, what a disaster! After a couple of false starts we ultimately found a modular system that we still use today. When I first looked at it everyone thought I was crazy because it was big and expensive, but I kept thinking how hard it was going to be to set up all the information. If we outgrew the system we would have to start all over again with an even bigger headache. Suzanne and Tim agreed it was the best way to go given the rate we were growing so we went ahead and bought the system. I was so glad. It worked perfectly and transformed customer service. We could answer customer's questions without having to look through reams of paper. Suzanne continued to spend more of her time with the computers and later added Human Recourses to her job description. In 1991 my sister came on board part time to help with our growing customer service department but she left shortly thereafter to raise her family. Later in 1996 Allyson, my new step daughter-in-law, joined customer service full time but she left in 1998 to have a baby, which makes me "Grammy Peg." Now we have Tara Elms as our customer service supervisor and all of our customers love her.

I broke all the rules when it came to hiring family and friends, a no-no in business. In 1992 it was getting harder for me to manage everything so my husband, Tim Seitz, joined the company full-time to take over sales. His enthusiasm for the business side of PKG enabled me to spend more time on the creative parts.

One of Tim's jobs was to manage our growing force of Sales Representatives. Sale Reps are an amazing group of people. Basically you hire them to manage a territory consisting of one or more states. They service your existing stores, find new customers, and take orders. They are independent, often representing several different companies, and work on commission. Many operate show rooms located in major cities where they display our products year round, along with the other lines they represent. It took a long time but over the years Tim was able to hire some of the best reps in the industry. Working together through the years we have become friends and developed great working relationships together.

Again I listened to what they had to say. They had tons of experience in the gift world and lots of good advice. One of Tim's favorite stories involves the person who contacted us and wanted to represent our line and just wouldn't give up. Tim figured with that kind of persistence how could we lose. Tim's instincts were correct and sure enough we continue to have a very profitable relationship.

Peggy Karr & Tim Seitz.

Because not many people were working in fused glass, there was very little information on how to do it and even less in the way of equipment. I was always trying to rig something or modify it to get it to work with my process. That, coupled with my limited funds, led to some really interesting solutions. In the beginning I used modified ceramic hobby kilns but they were slow and inconsistent. I came up with a new concept for a kiln and had someone build several for me. I thought he knew what I wanted but I was wrong. From the day they were delivered they didn't work correctly. He blamed me and of course I blamed him. He refused to come and work on them to correct the problems. In the end I spent so much time trying to fix them myself I knew more about how to build kilns then he did.

I had a lot of help from my brother-in-law, George Haversang. He started out helping on the weekends and in 1994 he joined the company full time. Coming from a background in electronics, his talents were invaluable. He also had the same passion for "building a better mouse trap" that I had. George stepped in with the electronics knowl-

edge and we were a force to be reckoned with. What started as a disaster worked out to be an asset. With all the time we spent working on the kilns we were able to come up with an even better plan to get them to work, something we never would have figured out without all that tinkering. Now our custom "Shuttle Kilns" work better than I thought they would.

George and I went on to make many more innovations together. Some of them were in the equipment needed to make our color; the custom work stations our decorator's use; and the special machine to clean our finished plates. We used to wash the finished pieces in a commercial dishwasher but they came out with spots. The washer couldn't get the powdered separator off properly and we had to additionally wipe each plate by hand. I guess you could say George and I are equipment addicts. It wasn't just limited to things we designed; it included things we just had to have.

I remember in 1991 we decided to buy our own forklift. We had been buying glass by the truckload and needed to have a way to get it off the truck without having to arrange for a forklift rental. The forklift we bought was used and we all had to take it for a test drive. And yes, we all had to try picking up the garbage dumpster and moving it around the parking lot. This was a big milestone for me. I felt like we were becoming a real business.

In September of 1992 I realized we were building our company buying glass enamel color from the sole provider in the United States. They singularly could completely shut down our production if they failed to deliver our colors. I dusted off my ceramics and chemistry books and began to formulate my own colors. This was the largest and most difficult task I've ever undertaken. Over the next few years and several thousand tests I was able to develop our own colors. I step back sometimes and am amazed at my perseverance back then. It hadn't occurred to me that the task I was undertaking was so monumental. I just kept plugging away at it and wouldn't give up. Initially I developed a pallet of thirty-two different colors that has grown to over fifty colors today. I try to add colors every year to enhance our new designs.

In 1993 I did my first "Signing Event" at a little shop called The Pan-Tree in Arlington, Virginia. I had gotten very friendly with the owner, Margo, because she was one of my first wholesale accounts. She said a lot of her customers would love to meet me so I packed up my electric engraving tool and took to the road. At signing events I personally sign and date plates purchased at that store. Sometimes I also add a short personal message such as "Happy Birthday Mom" to the plate.

I have a Love – Hate relationship with signing events. If I could snap my fingers and appear at the store and then pop back home I would do them all the time. I love people but I really hate travel and being away from home for long periods of time. I currently do about sixteen events a year;

that's all I can manage. One of my favorite locations is at a store called Borsheim's in Omaha Nebraska. I have been going there every year since 1994. It started out small but over the years it has grown tremendously. I think it must be the largest Signing Event in the U.S. Currently it takes me four days to sign thousands of plates for some of the nicest people. They all feel sorry for me because by the end of the event I can barely move my hand.

Peggy signing plates.

Our actual products have gone through a lot of transformations. The most important happened in 1996. Until then we had been cutting all of our stencils by hand. One of our new decorators, Billy, had computer graphics experience. He helped us computerize our artwork and we purchased a laser cutter to cut the stencils (more equipment). It had far reaching effects, including the ability to add details we were unable to cut by hand. Next we began to add different products. When I first started, I made plates in only a few sizes and they were all round. The first unusual thing I added was Seder Plates in 1989. I remembered some of my old cleaning clients were Jewish and complained they could never find any interesting Seder Plates, so I decided to give it a try. They were a big success but they were hard to make. In 1991 we introduced clocks, which were a great idea with a lot of problems. The metal hands would get bent. They only had to bend slightly and they would hang up on each other, causing the clock to stop working. The problem was compounded by the fact that the hands were large and covered the entire clock face. After a while we just gave up and retired them in 2000.

1992 was the year we started to make tables and ornaments. We actually made our own metal table bases because one of Tim's hidden talents was welding. As they became more and more popular, it became impossible for him to make them all. At first we trained one of our regular employees, a woman named Beth, how to make them and later a local decorative weld shop took over the task. Or-

naments came on the scene in 1992 and in 1993 L.L. Bean came to us and asked us to make them a custom ornament. They wanted 24, 000 of them! I wasn't sure we could handle the job but after some quick calculations we said yes. By the end of the task we all had a full appreciation of exactly how many ornaments 24,000 really was. There was a rabbit, a bear, a moose, and a loon.

Another great idea was Colorware, released in 1994. It was our version of dinnerware. It had a single color decorative border that was designed to coordinate with our plates. We added a couple of new sizes to give versatility to the line. We retired Colorware in 1998 for lack of sales but I think we were just slightly ahead of our time. We often talk about giving it a second chance. Also in 1994 we were struck by the "Pansy phenomenon." Sales of the Pansy pattern immediately went through the roof and it remained our best selling pattern for eight years. I didn't even design it; one of our regular designers, Donna, came up with the pattern.

In 1995 we figured if ornaments were good, larger roundels would be better. We made them in three sizes, each with a chain for hanging. Everyone seemed to lose interest in them, including the stores, so we discontinued them in 2000.

Another innovation in 1995 was starting to add some much-needed new shapes to the line. I started with two rectangles and in 1997 I added a 13" square and a heart, which required the purchase of a special shape cutter for the glass (more equipment). Fluted bowls came in 1998; the oval and tree were introduced in 2001; and lastly the fish and house in 2002. We experienced our only complete failure in 1999, when we introduced paper napkins to match our plates. We didn't do enough research and had no experience in this medium. They looked terrible and sales were even worse. I think we still have a lifetime supply in the warehouse.

In 2001 started the floral collectable series. The plates are limited to one year of production and I personally sign and number each one. They have been wonderfully successful. The hard part is trying to keep track of all those numbers. Was that 1104 or 1105? If you make a mistake with the engraving tool, you can't erase.

Lastly, one of our hidden successes has been our accessories. They are our metal and plastic stands, the lamp, and our table bases, which have helped to make our plates special. They turn an ordinary plate into a display piece or make it beautiful to serve on.

I know this is getting terribly long-winded, but I want to make sure I got in some of those little details that make things interesting. I also wanted to let you know that not everything was a success. You have to keep trying new things to keep everyone interested. Sometimes you hit a home run and sometimes you lay an egg. If you only focus on one good idea, people eventually get bored and move on to the next best thing and you will be left behind.

Since I'm talking about product, I thought it would be fun to talk about some of the more memorable places I have found my plates, often by accident. We were all working one day when a friend called out of breath and said, "you have to turn on the TV right now!" We got the TV on in time to see Richard Simmons using one of our twenty-inch platters to demonstrate how he made one of his gourmet salads. The camera spent most of the time on our platter and we were all tickled pink. Another time I was told by a friend to go and buy a new frozen dinner by "Le Menu". Imagine my surprise to find one of our plates on the box cover. Marinated slow-cooked beef mostly covered it but it was still my plate on millions of frozen food boxes. I was thrilled to find out our "Celebration" plate was selected as a gift to be given to the cast and crew of "Will & Grace." We specially engraved each piece with the show's title and date. We even have some plates in the palace of the Japanese Emperor. I suppose the most fun is when I'm at a party or someone's home and they bring out one of my plates to serve on and they haven't made the connection that I am the creator. It's great to get their off-hand comments about how much they love the plates before I "fess-up" to being the artist.

Coming up with the beautiful plates was easy compared to managing a business. One thing I knew for sure was I couldn't do it all by myself. I found the people to be among the most important and rewarding parts of running a business. I used to wonder, "Exactly what does a manager do?" because I had always been on the employee side of the fence. Besides working on a few committees I had never really managed a group of people. I was very good at fusing glass but now I needed a lot of help figuring out how to manage a business. I felt terribly responsible being in charge of all of these people and making sure I did the right thing. I would often hire consultants for their advice or to help me work through something I didn't understand.

In 1992 a good friend from the Fellowship, Mike Robinson, a retired executive from the industrial ceramics field came to help. At the time I didn't know it but he had been diagnosed with terminal cancer. After sailing around the world he chose to spend his last days helping me with my new business. He died in 1993; I still get tears in my eyes when I think about it. I miss him very much.

An even earlier mentor from the Fellowship was George Hays. He helped me stay on the straight and narrow. There were many times I almost got derailed and George would get me back on track. Questions about insurance, hiring policies, discipline, payroll, the list was endless. I had never worked in "Corporate America" so I just kept working it out and learning as I went along.

I started in 1987 with two employees and now employ over sixty. I hired two fabulous women, Estella and Christine, who started in the early 1990s as decorators and now they train and supervise our decorating department. It takes close to six months and tons of patience to completely train a new decorator. In 1996 my brother-in-law George's cousin, Ed Hamersma, came on board to manage the shipping department. When we were small it was fairly easy to put the plates in a box and get them out the door. As we grew and added more products and customers with special shipping instructions it required someone with a lot of attention to detail to keep everything straight. His wife, Donna, soon joined shipping and together they keep everything in the department running smoothly.

In 1999 I felt our art department needed someone with experience at the helm. Our little catalog had gotten a lot bigger and we were starting to do a lot more advertising. We needed to meet deadlines and better organize our design process. I called my good friend Yolanda who, at the time, was working in New York as an art director in the textile field, to ask if she might know someone. She said, "What about me?" It was a perfect fit. She brought with her a lifetime of experience and talent.

The last three important additions to the PKG staff came after we moved to Randolph but I thought it was best to talk about them here. The first is Lynda Portelli. She came in 2001 as a much-needed addition to our marketing staff. She has enormous enthusiasm, drive, and a vast amount of experience in the gift industry. She has been pivotal in developing our advertising and promotional programs. The second is Rick Pietrzak. He joined us in 2002 and manages our production staff.

Again, we needed someone who had experience to bring order out of chaos. In the beginning everyone just came and went with separate schedules. That worked when there were only twenty people, but when there are sixty, it becomes chaos when you are trying to plan and run production. No one wanted to change but Rick came in with determination and now there is order.

Lastly in 2003 Tim's son, Derek Seitz, joined and started training to become our Chief Operating Officer and take over the day to day running of the company. The best story I can tell about Derek took place back in 1984, before Tim and I were involved. He was about thirteen years old and full of trouble. His family were members of the Unitarian Fellowship and came regularly on Sundays. He had managed to sneak into my studio while I was coming and going one Sunday. I had errands to run so I closed up my studio and left, locking both Derek and his friend in. When someone finally found them, they had to pry the door off its hinges to get them out. How could I imagine back then that he would someday run my business? Derek came from a corporate background in engineering and computer science.

Tim and I have started to look toward the future so we decided to get the next generation onboard. Derek brings a fresh approach and tons of energy. Running a business takes a certain kind of talent. You just can't rule with an iron fist. One has to be able to take the bull by the horns without getting his nose out of joint. If anyone can do it, Derek can.

Derek Seitz and Lynda Portelli.

Michael Karr and Suzanne Farese.

As a group we love to have a good time. In October of 1993 we hit our first million in sales and we all drank way too much champagne. I remember we used to get dressed for Halloween. Diane, one of our designers, came as a psychotic. She kept acting stranger and stranger all day. We all thought something was really wrong until she couldn't stand it any longer and burst out laughing. We all work really hard up until Christmas so we shut down for the week between Christmas and New Year's every year. We usually have some kind of holiday celebration. When we all get cleaned up I sometimes don't recognize everyone without their work cloths on. Many of our production staff wear white coveralls to protect their clothes at work, making the distinction even harder. We call them "Bunny Suits" after someone hung a cottontail on their rear end.

One of my favorite things is our company celebration lunches. They cover anything from birthdays to meeting our monthly goals. People bring in all sorts of wonderful homemade dishes and we get to sit down together and acknowledge our successes, both personal and company. It's what helps to make us a good team.

I think everyone remembers where they were on 9/11. Tim and I had taken off in a plane from Newark Airport one hour before the terrorists. We were on our way to a signing event in Omaha, Nebraska. Everyone was frantic wondering if we were on one of the ill-fated planes. After several tense hours in the airport we were finally able to get through to home and let everyone know we were safe. We went on to do the signing event, unable to get home, and the store donated all the proceeds that weekend to the Red Cross. As many others did, we all pulled together after the 9/11 tragedy. After the weekend was over we decided to design a special flag plate and arranged with all our retailers to donate all the profits to the United Way. It was a particularly busy Christmas rush and we were already putting in lots of overtime. We all worked double time getting the plates out and were able to raise $172, 000 for the 9/11 fund. I still can't believe it.

One of the comments I get from people who come to visit the factory is how enthusiastic and dedicated the staff is. Through the years we have accomplished a lot together. I have learned the intricate skills needed to manage a successful business. I have also learned that people are my most valuable asset. There are so many people at Peggy Karr Glass who have contributed their talents and hard work, it's impossible to name them all. I am so proud of everyone; I couldn't have done it without them.

## WASHINGTON STREET, RANDOLPH, NEW JERSEY 2000 - PRESENT

When we started in Cedar Knolls we had 6, 000 square feet and about twelve employees. When we left we had 17, 500 square feet and over fifty employees. We were like sardines in a can. If one person stood still it was only a matter of minutes before they were in someone's way. We started our real estate search in 1997 and didn't find our new home until 1999. I shopped for our new home just like any other red-blooded American woman; I looked at and compared every building available in Morris County. We even nicknamed some of them. There was "Thunder Dome", a reference to the dungeon-like environment in the Mel Gibson movie. There was also "Beyond Thunder Dome" where the building had an open pit in the warehouse area with this green floating slime. I didn't want to know what it was. After endless searching we found the perfect building in Randolph. The location was ideal; most of our employees were from the area. It was for sale and we negotiated a great price. Two weeks before we were to close, the owner decided not to sell. I was crushed. I even got on the phone and begged, but with no luck. I had fallen in love with the Randolph area.

There had been one other building in Randolph that I felt was too large for us but had lots of potential. The owner was willing to divide the space if we wanted. We walked around and measured and no matter how we looked at it there just wasn't a good way to divide it. With no other options available I did some hard calculations and made the owner an offer to rent the whole building. I now have 60, 000 square feet to play with. It is beyond huge; you could train for a marathon in there. We moved over the Christmas - New Year's holiday in 1999. This time there were big flatbed trucks and experienced moving men but it was still utter chaos for weeks. Nothing could be found. We had lots of renovations done before we moved, including installing new heat in part of the warehouse. Well, of course it wasn't ready and the temperature plummeted into the teens. When we finally got settled it was fantastic. Some of our original hobby kilns had still been in production in Cedar Knolls but none of them survived the move. We built more of our custom "shuttle kilns" to bring the total to fourteen.

With all our new space our productivity improved immediately. We were able to layout the work flow more efficiently. Everyone had space to set up their own work area and not be in someone's way. Instead of putting out little forest fires all day, I got to spend more time designing and improving our glass. One thing I had always wanted was a place I could do all my experiments. Up until now most of my things were spread around in boxes and cabinets, but now I have been able to set up my work area and have everything right where I need it.

In 2000 we entered the cyber world and launched our web site, peggykarrglass.com. The next year the site went interactive and people could search for stores in their area. In 2003 we added a business-to-business site that allows our reps

and stores to interact with our main computer to place orders or check on their status. Now we spend a lot of time talking about "fire walls" and "viruses".

We opened our outlet store in 2001 and Derek's wife, Allyson, came back to get the store started. It's terrific and we even give tours through the factory. Our new home is working out just fine. I am, however, finding that there is one thing that is true; given time you will acquire enough stuff to fill all available space. It's scary when I think we have sixty thousand square feet to play with. If we have to move again, I'm going on vacation and I won't come back until it's done.

People often ask if I ever thought it would get this big. The answer is no. Once I got PKG started it seemed to take on a life of its own. I have found that success is twenty percent good ideas and eighty percent hard work. The reward for me is being able to fulfill my passion to create. The bonus is getting to share Peggy Karr Glass with everyone.

Patty Voeglie, our Factory Outlet Store Manager, inside the entrance, 2004.

A view inside our outlet store.

Third location in Randolph, 2000.

Staff photo 2003

Before we follow a plate from beginning to end I need to give you some background information. I will describe all the materials, equipment, and processes needed.

Collage of enamels, sifters, stencils, color chips, and 11 inch pansy plate.

## DESIGN

Before you can make a plate you need to design it. When I first started our designs were very simple. I chose simple country animals on a checkerboard theme which were easy to design and easy to enamel. Today our designs are very complicated and it takes a long time to teach someone all the techniques needed to be one of our artisans.

Among the main challenges with enameled glass are the bubbles. Every piece has them. They form when air gets trapped between the two layers of clear glass in the firing process.

The trick is to learn how to minimize them. Through years of trial and error we have learned what works and what doesn't in design. Most of our designers started as decorators, so they have an intimate understanding of the enameling process. That knowledge, coupled with our basic set of guidelines, allows us to create the beautiful pieces you see in this book.

Every year we create new patterns and retire old ones and we often rely on suggestions given to us by our customers. Their feedback is invaluable. Not every design makes it into production because often what looks good on paper is a disaster in glass. Either the colors don't work, there are too many bubbles or it just plain doesn't look good. Once a design is accepted it goes through a long process of testing to make sure we can reproduce it successfully. Every now and then we make a mistake and a design has a high failure rate after it has been put into production. If we can't fix it we have to retire it early.

David Switzer starting with a rough sketch.

Diane Johnston designing in the computer.

## STENCILS

Once you have the design, you need a set of stencils to apply the color. Stencils are made from cardboard and have instructions describing what colors to use and how to apply them. The stencils are cut out to correspond to each different color in the pattern and there can be up to ten stencils per design. They work just like the stencils you would use to stencil your walls or decorate a card. In the beginning we cut them all by hand using X-acto knives. This was a very tedious process, often leaving your hand very sore and there was also a limit to how much small detail you could cut by hand. If we needed to rework a design it would take a week to cut all the new stencils. We worried if there was ever any disaster we would never be able to duplicate all of our patterns from memory. One of our new decorators, Billy, had computer graphic experience and it wasn't long before we were entering our designs into a computer and humming along using a laser to cut our stencils. It was the most liberating experience. It opened the door to new design possibilities by enabling us to add the detail we wanted and make changes easily and quickly for production.

Another aspect of our design department is custom work. We do everything from creating a design from the ground up to translating someone else's artwork into glass. We get many requests for a wide variety of things like landmarks, skylines, buildings, high school logos, commemorative events, artist paintings, the list goes on. In the beginning we spent so much time working out all the problems we never seemed to make any money; but now, with all of our experience, we are able to consistently create a design that works well.

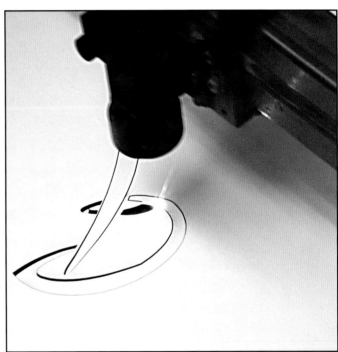

A view of the laser cutter close up.

One of our custom jobs for Clinton, Missouri.

We currently cut over twenty different sizes and shapes of glass, all by hand. We use some machines that score the glass but it all must be broken out by hand. We have some of the most amazing glasscutters who are incredible to watch. Years ago I was as fast as they were but now I could never keep up. We even looked into a water jet to cut the glass but our glasscutters were faster and more efficient.

All of the glass is washed before it is decorated. Dirt and fingerprints will be permanently fired into the glass if they are not removed. In the past we cleaned all the glass by hand. At one point it was a rotating task and the person who got stuck with the job that day was called "The Happy Helper". Now we have a machine that washes and dries the glass in just a few seconds.

Taking a finished stencil out of the laser cutter.

Alberto Hiciano cutting glass circles.

Billy Brisley marking a stencil with decorating instructions.

# GLASS

Not all glass is the same. It may look the same but beyond the main ingredients of sand (silica), soda ash, and lime there are a lot of other things you can add to glass to give it other properties. We look for glass that, when reheated, retains its clarity and shine. Glass also changes from factory to factory based on the raw materials available in each area so we have to be very particular when we order it. In the beginning I would order it by the case and now we order it by the tractor-trailer load.

Javier Arias cutting glass trees with the shape cutter.

Breaking out the tree shape after it has been scored on the shape cutter.

Drilling holes for our glass ornaments before they are decorated.

Milton Argueta washing the cut glass before it is decorated.

## COLOR

The colors are an area of the business of which I am extremely proud. When I started Peggy Karr Glass there was only one manufacturer of glass enamels in the United States. Their quality and availability was limited. As PKG grew, I was concerned that if anything happened to the manufacturer I was out of business. So, I decided to make my own enamels. How hard could it be? The colors had to match the thermal expansion of the base glass and melt with a minimum of bubbles at the right temperature without running. It was a taller order than I expected, but I was like a dog with a bone.

After thousands of experiments I was finally able to produce all of our own colors, including red, which is one of the hardest colors to produce. The color is carefully ground to the consistency of powdered sugar and applied dry with small hand held sifters ranging in size from 1/4 inch to about 3 inches in diameter. It takes a lot of expert hand-eye coordination to apply the colors evenly. I also make a special silk screening ink we use to create black line detail in our plates. The color is screened onto the underside of the top piece of glass and can be used to achieve fine black lines. We have used this technique for our Premier Series, clock numbers, and special logos. Making our own colors allows us to carefully control our quality and have a much wider selection than was previously available. We are currently working with over fifty different colors and I try to add new ones each year.

Hector Torres processing some of the ingredients for our colors.

Mixing the ingredients for our colors in a cone blender.

## DECORATING

Our largest group of employees is our decorating staff. They are the people who carefully sift all the enamel colors onto the glass. It takes months of training before a decorator is proficient enough to enamel all of our designs consistently. Many of our designs have up to ten stencils with lots of shading so a complicated fourteen inch design can take up to twenty minutes to complete. The simpler designs and smaller sizes go faster and of course the larger ones can take longer. It takes a lot of hand-eye coordination, attention to detail, and patience to become one of our expert artisans.

Yolanda Fundora and Estela Switzer discussing a new pattern before putting it in production.

Finished color.

Christine Ricucci and Lilly Moreno going over a new custom design.

David Switzer silk screening glass with our custom black ink.

## MOLDS

Since all the glass starts out flat, you have to have a way to form it in the kiln. As the glass is fired it softens and takes on the shape of whatever it is sitting on via gravity. I designed all the molds we use in the firing process. In the beginning they were all made by hand one at a time from clay. My past experience as a potter from college came in handy. I worked hard to get graceful shapes that were glass friendly in the kiln. Later we added stainless steel forms modeled from our clay molds. It was much easier than making them one at a time in clay, plus they don't break when you drop them. The glass will stick to everything as it melts so all the molds must be coated with a separator. We sift a special powder onto all the molds every time we fire them to keep the glass from sticking. The powdered separator is what leaves the pebbled finish on the bottom of all our plates.

Clay and metal molds we use in production.

Clay molds drying on a rack before they are fired.

## KILNS

The very first kiln I used was an old kiln from my ceramic days. It was okay, but it was slow and the temperature was uneven. It may have been good for firing pots but it wasn't designed to fire glass. I designed some changes into regular ceramic kilns and had some local manufacturers make them for me. Again, they were better but they were still slow and uneven. I decided to go back to the drawing board. I came up with an entirely new kiln concept and had someone else produce it but there were lots of problems. At about the same time, my brother-in-law, George, came to work with me. We started to rebuild the new kiln from the ground up. I provided the concept and state of the art insulation materials while George made them work with his electronic wizardry. They have been through three generations and now our "shuttle kilns" work like a dream. We are able to fire the glass quickly and evenly with a minimum of energy.

Firing clay molds in a ceramic kiln before they can be used in production.

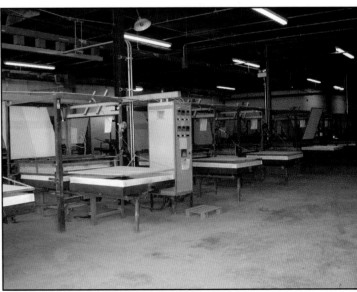

View of the kiln area.

Left to right: Gilbert Lorenzo, Rick Pietrzak, and George Haversang discussing a new kiln base.

Miguel Benitez cleaning the glass before loading it into the kiln.

## FIRING

The kilns are carefully run with state-of-the-art electronic controllers that fire the glass with very sensitive time and temperature profiles. All of our plates consist of a top and bottom piece of glass with the color in the middle. The decorated piece is fired to about 1600 degrees Fahrenheit and at that temperature the two pieces of glass melt together, the color melts into the glass, and the glass gets soft enough to take on the contour of the mold. This process encases the color in glass, which protects it from fading and wearing off forever, making it food and dishwasher safe. The only exception is our ornaments, which are only one piece of glass with the color on top. The specially designed programs and kilns fire our glass consistently with the best possible results. Much as we would like every kiln to be exactly the same they all have little differences. Our kiln operators have gotten to know all their eccentricities and plan accordingly. It is their job to load, program, fire, and unload all the glass. Sometimes in the summer the temperatures can exceed 100 degrees in the kiln area, which makes their job doubly hard.

Miguel loading the decorated glass into the kiln.

Felix Gonzalez programming the kiln.

George Fortuna and Francisco Vasquez washing the finished plates after they have been fired.

## QUALITY CONTROL

After all our plates are finished they are carefully inspected to make sure they are first quality. Each piece is then signed with the company initials PKG and the year with a diamond engraver. They then apply our little "Made in the USA" sticker and are ready to go into inventory. Over the years they have developed a keen eye and give lots of feedback to the decorators and art department concerning problems and ways to improve.

Fabio Alonso checking the finished plates for quality.

Eric Marrero signing the plates with a diamond engraver after they have been inspected.

## BOXES

All of our plates come in one of our distinctive "pizza" boxes. Back in 1987 we used to wrap all the plates in bubble wrap. It was a pain in the neck trying to hold down the plastic and work the tape gun at the same time. One day we were all sitting around having pizza for lunch. We looked at the box and then looked at our plates and the light bulb went on. I called the pizza guy and asked him where he got his boxes. Well, lots of phone calls later I could order pizza boxes with "Fresh Hot Pizza" printed on them but none that were plain white.

Before I can finish this story I have to tell another. When I first started it was almost impossible to get someone to come to my little studio to sell me packing materials. They all wanted to know how many truckloads I wanted, except for Kenny. He graciously came to my fellowship address and climbed the three flights of stairs to sell me one bundle of boxes and two bags of peanuts. We still buy all our packing materials from Kenny, now by the truckload. Kenny likes to tell our story to new sales people in his business saying, "You never know."

Needless to say Kenny was a hero and found us our "pizza" boxes.

Ed Hamersma placing a plate in the folded box.

Packing a master carton.

## CUSTOMER SERVICE

Our customer service representatives are the link between PKG and the outside world. Their main job is to take and process orders but listening to them on the phone tells another story. They help customers make decisions, listen to complaints, sort out problems, and develop close relationships with a lot of our customers. They keep track of who wanted what and whether or not it's paid for. They play a vital role in keeping the lines of communication open between PKG and our customers.

## SHIPPING

Shipping is sometimes the forgotten department but they perform an important role at PKG. They are the last to see the plates before they get put into a box and shipped out. They make sure each order goes out correctly and on time. If something is missing for an order they will make sure someone from decorating makes it before the end of the day. It's a testament to our shipping department that our orders arrive complete, on time, and unbroken.

Donna Hamersma putting the ribbon loop on and boxing ornaments.

Our customer service staff: Robin Cotter, Tara Elms, and Daniela Podhorodecki.

# FOLLOWING THE PANSY BOWL FROM START TO FINISH

1. Hand cutting the glass before decorating.

2. Lining up the glass to the design.

3. Sifting the powdered colors onto the glass.

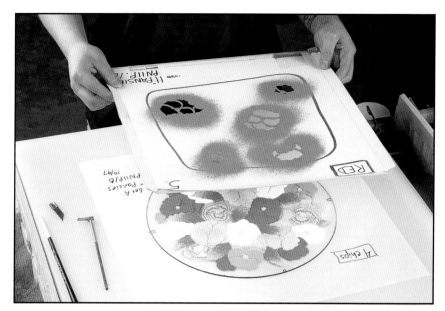

4. Carefully lifting one of the many stencils.

5. Placing the second piece of glass over the design.

6. Coating the mold with a powdered separator.

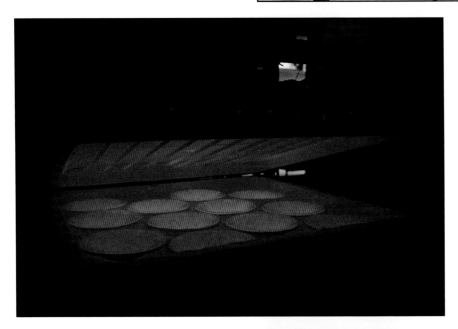

7. Loading the decorated glass onto a mold in the kiln.

8. Firing the glass and color to about 1600 degrees Fahrenheit.

9. The glass after it has been fired.

10. Signing the plate with a diamond engraver.

11. Applying our "Made in the USA" sticker.

12. Placing the plate in our custom "pizza" box for shipping.

## CHAPTER FIVE

QUALITIES

Example of our signatures. First is the company initials and year found on every first quality plate. Second is Peggy's signature found only on special plates.

## What to Look For

There are a lot of different ways you can work glass in a kiln. Since I started over twenty years ago, I have seen some incredible new artists and techniques. Just surf the Internet under fused, warm, or kiln-fired glass and you will be amazed.

I have given you a good general overview of fused enameled glass in previous chapters. Peggy Karr Glass has gone through a lot of change over the years and experience has been the best teacher. When I see some of our early pieces I am amazed at how much our designs and quality have improved over time. You can see some of the changes looking through our patterns in this book. They are arranged by the years they were produced so it is easy to see the progression.

There are a lot of other fused enameled glass artists out there. Some of them sell nationally and some are local artists who create out of their homes. Most of them have their own style and, until recently, almost all were made in the USA. With the growing popularity of fused glass, other countries are entering the marketplace. I would like to help educate you in what to look for in enameled glass, especially Peggy Karr Glass.

### SIGNATURE

The best way you can make sure you are purchasing a first quality Peggy Karr Glass piece is to look for the signature. It usually appears at about 5 o'clock on the outside rim of the piece. It is engraved with an electric hand-held diamond engraver and looks white. If the plate has been handled, the oil from your fingers can make the signature "disappear". Simply clean the piece and the signature will reappear. Over the years we have signed them differently. In the beginning, all the plates were signed "P Karr". In 1996 we add three initials after the signature to indicate the Designer, "P Karr / SKA". If the plate had no initials during this time, I designed it. In the year 2000 we changed the signature to "PKG '00" (indicating Peggy Karr Glass and the year).

In the early years I signed most of the plates; now our quality control department signs them. Some of the signatures were done quite small and are hard to find; however, if there is NO Peggy Karr Glass signature, it is either second quality or the work of another artist. The only plates I currently sign personally are either from signing events I attend throughout the country or the annual collectible plates, which I sign and number. You know you have my signature if it appears "Peggy Karr followed by the year". At signing events I will also personalize pieces with inscriptions such as, "Merry Christmas Love, Mom & Dad". I use the same engraving tool used to sign the plates.

## BUBBLES

There will ALWAYS be bubbles. This happens when the piece is fired and air gets trapped between the two layers of glass. PKG has worked very hard to keep them to a minimum. The bubbles do not weaken the glass, but they do not look attractive if they are too large.

## HAZING

If a whitish haze appears on the surface of a new piece, there can be several reasons. Either it was over-fired in the kiln or the glass used was not of good quality. If it is a piece purchased second-hand, it could be lime build-up from hard water in a dishwasher or very caustic dishwashing liquid. If it is lime build-up, it can be removed with any lime-cleaning product. As all window glass is not the same, PKG uses special glass to ensure that hazing does not occur. If we over-fire a piece, it is considered a second and sold as such.

## CRAZING

This appears as small cracks running through the color and happens when you use color that is not compatible with the glass, which weakens it. The piece is more likely to break due to thermal shock or light impact. Do not put a piece with crazing in the dishwasher or microwave. Except for some early pieces done before 1990, all Peggy Karr Glass does not have this problem.

## RUNNY COLOR

High Fire Glass Enamels are available in very few places in the United States. PKG makes all of our own colors so we can carefully control our quality and color pallet. Other artist must rely on colors that are available commercially. If the colors are runny, it is either poor quality enamels or the piece was over-fired in the kiln.

## BAD RED

This occurs when the red starts to turn brown. Red is singularly the most difficult color to work with. I often wish I had a degree in Ceramic Engineering so I could better understand the chemistry and improve the color. Mostly

we just chalk it up to God and try a new batch. We will not pass a plate if the red is too dark.

## ROUGH-UNFINISHED EDGES

This occurs when either the edges are not fused all the way, showing the two separate pieces of glass, or the edges are rough, indicating the piece was over-fired. Neither will effect using the piece but I feel it is important to make every piece to a high quality standard.

## SURFACE TEXTURE

All fused glass has a texture or pattern on the back of the glass. When the glass is fired in the kiln it becomes very sticky at fusing temperatures. All the molds must be coated with a separating material so the glass won't stick to the mold. Also at fusing temperatures the glass will take on the pattern of anything it is resting on, including the separating material. At PKG we sift a ceramic powder onto our molds that leaves the pebbled finish on the back of our plates. Some artists paint the separator on, giving a different finish to their work.

## SECONDS

Each piece of Peggy Karr Glass is inspected carefully before we sign it, indicating it is first quality. We have an outlet store located at our factory where we sell our seconds. Years ago we also used to have special sales three times a year. Be careful when purchasing pieces on E-Bay or at second hand stores, as you may not be getting a signed first quality piece. Look for the signature to be sure you are getting first quality Peggy Karr Glass.

## CUSTOM

Through the years Peggy Karr Glass has made hundreds of Custom Plates and designs. They are too numerous for me to name. We have produced things in all our different sizes and shapes, including ornaments. We have done everything from designing something from scratch to reproducing someone else's artwork. We have also customized some of our already existing plates by changing the colors, adding a logo or special date. When we make these plates, we often don't sign them by request of the customer, so you won't find our company signature. If you come across something, the best ways to tell if it is one of ours are by our distinctive shapes and colors. If it matches, it may be one of our custom plates.

In closing, "Beauty is in the eye of the beholder". What appeals to one person may not appeal to another. Peggy Karr Glass tries to create a wide variety of patterns that will appeal to a broad range of people. In an effort to improve our quality and designs, we introduce many new patterns every year as well as retire the old ones. Fusing has been a continual journey of evolution and discovery for me.

## CHAPTER SIX

DESIGNERS

Our current design staff. From left to right: Peggy Karr, David Switzer, Billy Brisley, Diane Johnston, and Yolanda Fundora. 2004

When I started Peggy Karr Glass I was very lucky to hire some very talented artist to decorate the plates. It didn't take me long to recognize their other abilities. I encouraged their creativity and allowed interested employees to try their hand at designing. It worked out fabulously. The designs were varied and gave the line a much broader appeal. Many of those people are still with me today. Others have left to pursue various careers.

In the beginning, all the plates were signed "P Karr". In 1996, we added three initials after the signature to indicate the Designer, "P Karr / SKA". If the plate had no initials during that time, the design was mine. In the year 2000, we changed the signature to "PKG '00" (indicating Peggy Karr Glass and the year). Listed below are all of our designers and their "initials, " if applicable. I have included resumes of our top designers, arranged in order by their start date. At the end is a list of employees who also tried their hand at designing, creating a few patterns each.

## SUZY ARVIDSON, "SKA"

Born in Alabama, Suzy Arvidson was raised in a military family, traveled the United States, and ultimately landed in New Jersey. Suzy began working at Peggy Karr Glass in 1989, where her early responsibilities included shipping, production, and sweeping floors! When she was given her chance at designing, there was no turning back. Soon after, Suzy was named art director for the company. Suzy helped guide the direction of the design staff and develop their talent. She created many designs, including the original Tropical Fish, Gardening, Rabbits, and Rainforest. Suzy managed the custom design area as well, coordinating custom products for clients such as Porsche, The National Archives, and St. Hubert's Animal Shelter. She also directed the corporate identity of PKG, designing the logo and developing promotional materials such as catalogs, fliers, advertisements, and exhibit booths. Fortunate to work with a very gifted group of artists, Suzy helped PKG to become the fine organization that it is today.

Suzy's education encompassed years at different colleges, culminating with a BFA in design from William Paterson College (University now). A perpetual student, she has continued her education with additional coursework over the years.

Suzy left PKG in 1998 and is currently promotions manager at Rutgers University Press, a non-profit publishing company. She is currently working on her first children's book.

## DONNA ORSINI DESJADON, "DOD"

Donna began working at PKG in 1989. She started as a decorator and the company soon promoted her to lead decorator. Her enameling work was outstanding in both quality and workmanship. She became one of the first supervisors in the growing Decorating Department. One of her main responsibilities was training the new decorators in glass enameling techniques.

Donna began designing in 1990, starting with a shell pattern. She was responsible for several of PKG's top patterns, including Saint Nick, Chili's, and Pansy (which has been our best selling pattern ever).

Donna graduated from Fairleigh Dickinson University. She was a Floral Designer before joining PKG and left the company in 2002. Her sister, Dana, currently works at PKG.

## DAVID SWITZER, "DTS"

David Switzer came to Peggy Karr Glass in late 1989. He started in production, which involved all aspects of making the final product. He cut glass, enameled the plates, and loaded the kilns. David was one of the first people in Quality Control. He even spent time in color production, making him one of our most versatile employees.

David was an art major at San Marin College in California and continued his education at the Pratt Institute. He worked as a freelance illustrator from 1984-1987 and was a member of the Board of Trustees of the Somerset Art Association from 1985-1988. He has won numerous art awards in New Jersey, and took part in the Society of Illustrators Humor Show in 1987. He also worked as an art conservator in the late 1980s.

David remains an active member of PKG as a full time designer.

## SALLI-ANN MULLEN, "SAM"

Salli-Ann Mullen was employed at PKG from 1989-1996, with primary duties in Quality Control. Salli-Ann joined PKG after reading an article about PKG in the newspaper. She designed several patterns during her stay, most of which had children's themes. Salli has a degree in Electrical Engineering from Penn State University, much to her dismay, as she was advised by her mother to pursue a career in something more secure than the arts. The advice hasn't stopped her from continuing on her creative paths.

Salli has since retired and enjoys time spent in her garden and with her grandchildren.

## DIANE JOHNSTON, "DCJ"

Diane Johnston began working at Peggy Karr Glass in 1990, coming with a background in the decorative arts. She started work as a decorator, but quickly became a designer, which is still her full time position.

Diane attended The School of Visual Arts in Manhattan. She later worked as a studio painter for Karl Mann & Associates, a design and decorative arts company. During that time Diane did freelance color separation for ABC Textiles.

In the early 1980s she moved to Washington, D.C., where she worked with Ed Haddad, an antiques appraiser. From there she met Bill Adair of Gold Leaf Studios and became a conservationist, gilding works in the collections of the White House and the Smithsonian, as well as private clients. She also continued her freelance artwork, doing jobs for Roche, Silver Burdett Books, and The Washington Post, to name a few.

Upon her return to New Jersey in the latter part of the 1980s, Diane continued in the decorative arts field as a muralist and trompe l'oeil painter. She then moved into ceramics by doing murals on tile that led to her receiving commissions by private collectors to do both small and large-scale works.

As a PKG designer Diane has been responsible for creating many of the patterns in this book. If you look carefully, you'll find an "E" hidden in each of her patterns in honor of her daughter Emily.

## BILLY BRISLEY

Billy Brisley began his career with Peggy Karr Glass in September of 1996 as a part time decorator after being employed as a designer for a clothing label company and Art Director for a Las Vegas based casino publishing company.

With much of his past employment utilizing the computer and many software applications, he took a look at the art department. We were still doing all of our drawing and stencil cutting by hand at that time. In the winter of 1997 Billy came to work full time and took on the job of computerizing the Art Department. He revolutionized our stencil cutting with the use of a laser cutter.

Today Billy manages the stencil department and designs when he can. He is a graduate of the Philadelphia School of Printing & Advertising and attended The Philadelphia School of the Arts for computer graphics. He is also an accomplished studio potter. His main interest, however, is the theater. He spent his early years performing in Las Vegas shows as a dancer/acrobat. He now spends all his free time performing in community productions or directing choreography.

## YOLANDA FUNDORA

Yolanda Fundora was born in Havana, Cuba, but spent most of her childhood and teenage years in Manhattan. She attended the College of Visual and Performing Arts, Syracuse University, majoring in painting and printmaking. After a decade long stint as a rock and roll musician in various all women bands, she moved to San Juan, Puerto Rico to reacquaint herself with both Caribbean culture and her native tongue. She also sought to seriously pursue her fine art career. She had her first one woman show in 1983.

She was deeply involved in Mujeres Artistas de Puerto Rico throughout the eighties and exhibited in galleries and museums of the Caribbean, New York City, and Washington, D.C. Her work forms part of many private and public collections, most important of which is the acquisition by the Museum of Contemporary Art of Puerto Rico of "Esperando a Carmen Luisa", a Prismacolor self-portrait, for the museum's permanent collection.

During her time in San Juan, Yolanda worked in the advertising field. In the late 1980s Yolanda was hired as an illustrator and product designer for a dual based New York gift design studio. In 1991 the studio needed to move all operations to New York City. Eventually Yolanda and another designer founded their own studio offering illustration, surface, and 3-dimensional product design, including textiles and toys. Among the clients she has worked for are Enesco, Liz-at-Home, Ebeling & Reuss, Towle Silver, and Dept 56, to name only a few. She has also worked in-house as a textile designer for Concord Fabrics and V.I.P. as a freelance illustrator and designer

Yolanda Fundora joined Peggy Karr Glass as Art Director in 1999. During her years as Art Director she further computerized the department so we now produce the art-work for all of our printed materials in house. Her many designs have helped greatly to add diversity to our line. She has recently reduced her hours to part time and is presently pursuing a renewed fine art career in digital printmaking and has plans for several shows, including a one woman show in San Juan, Puerto Rico in October 2004.

## OTHER DESIGNERS/EMPLOYEES

Mary Kay Mickiewicz, "MKM", 1987-1992
Carol Haskel, 1987-1989
Chris Krupinski, 1988-1989
Pat Provost, "PNP", 1988-1990
Mary Ellen Whiteley, 1989-1990
Darren Bizzel, 1989-1996
Jeff Wallace, 1990-2001
Mary Pat Povilaitis, 1991-1994
Beth Ziolkowski, "BE", 1991-1997
Vanessa Barresse, 1991-1993
Andy Barresse, "AB", 1992-1994
Stacy Rios, 1995-1996

Ann Mallory, 1993, was not an employee but a good friend and professional ceramic designer who created "Tribal".

Early design staff. Left to right: Donna Desjadon, Diane Johnston, David Switzer, Peggy Karr, Beth Ziolkoski, Suzy Arvidson. 1995.

Harvest Fruit pattern showing some of the many ways it was available.

## CHAPTER SEVEN

Peggy Karr Glass has become more and more collectable over the years. Below is a rating based on production quantities. The information after the pattern names in the "Designware" sections arranged by year will have this rating following "Availability". Numbers are based on an "average" for any one size within a pattern over the entire life of that pattern. Some patterns were only available for one year while others have been in production for many years. There may be a few more or less of one size than another within a pattern. Another point to remember is Peggy Karr Glass grew over time. Many of the patterns from the early years are rated as rare. This is not because they were unpopular but because our production capabilities and marketing efforts were limited back then.

## RARE
Less than 500 pieces per size were made on average. Extremely hard to find.

## LIMITED
Between 500-1000 pieces per size were made on average. Hard to find.

## AVERAGE
Between 1000-2500 pieces per size were made on average. Easy to find.

## COMMON
Between 2500-5000 pieces per size were made on average. Very easy to find.

## NUMEROUS
Over 5000 pieces per size were made on average. Extremely easy to find.

# ACTUAL PLATE SIZES

We name our plate sizes by their original glass size before firing. After firing the glass usually shrinks from the size stated except for the 11" plates, which actually start out as 11 1/2". Below are all the true dimensions for the sizes listed.

| | |
|---|---|
| 06" Plate: | 5 5/8" in diameter, 1/2" deep |
| 08" Plate: | 7 3/4" in diameter, 1/2" deep |
| 10" Plate*: | 9 3/4" in diameter, 1/2" deep |
| 11" Plate: | 11 1/4" in diameter, 1/2" deep |
| 14" Platter: | 13 5/8" in diameter, 1" deep |
| 16" Platter: | 15 3/4" in diameter, 1" deep |
| 20" Platter: | 19 1/2" in diameter, 1 1/2" deep |
| 18" Oval: | 12 3/4" x 17 3/4", 1" deep |
| 14" Seder: | 13 3/4" in diameter, 1 1/8" deep |

| | |
|---|---|
| 10" Tray: | 6 3/4" x 9 3/4", 1/2" deep |
| 14" Tray: | 7 3/4" x 13 3/4", 1/2" deep |
| 16" Tray: | 16 1/4" x 9 1/2", 1 1/2" deep |
| 10" Square: | 9 5/8" x 9 5/8", 1" deep |
| 13" Square: | 12 1/2" x 12 1/2", 1 1/2" deep |

| | |
|---|---|
| 10" Heart: | 9 1/2" high x 10" wide, 3/4" deep |

| | |
|---|---|
| 14" Tree: | 14" high x 12 1/2" wide, 1" deep |
| 11" Fish: | 8 1/2" high x 11 1/4" wide, 1" deep |
| 12" House: | 12" high x 10 1/2" wide, 1" deep |

| | |
|---|---|
| 06" Bowl*: | 5 1/2" in diameter, 1" deep |
| 08" Bowl*: | 7 1/2" in diameter, 1 1/2" deep |
| 09" Bowl: | 8 3/8" in diameter, 1 1/2" deep |
| 10" Bowl*: | 9 1/4" in diameter, 1 1/2" deep |
| 11" Bowl: | 10 3/4" in diameter, 2" deep |
| 14" Bowl: | 13 1/8" in diameter, 2 1/2" deep |
| 16" Bowl: | 15 1/8" in diameter, 2 1/2" deep |

| | |
|---|---|
| 09" Flute: | 8 3/8" in diameter, 1 1/2" deep |
| 11" Flute: | 10 3/4" in diameter, 2" deep |

| | |
|---|---|
| 16" Tabletop: | 16 1/2" x 16 1/2", 3/8" thick |
| 20" Tabletop: | 20 1/2" in diameter, 3/8" thick |

| | |
|---|---|
| 09" Clock: | 8 7/8" in diameter, battery operated works |
| 11" Clock: | 11 1/4" in diameter, battery operated works |

| | |
|---|---|
| 6" Roundel: | 5 7/8" in diameter, flat |
| 8" Roundel: | 7 7/8" in diameter, flat |
| 11" Roundel: | 11 1/4" in diameter, flat |

| | |
|---|---|
| 03" Ornament: | 3 3/8" in diameter, flat |

*Available in colorware only

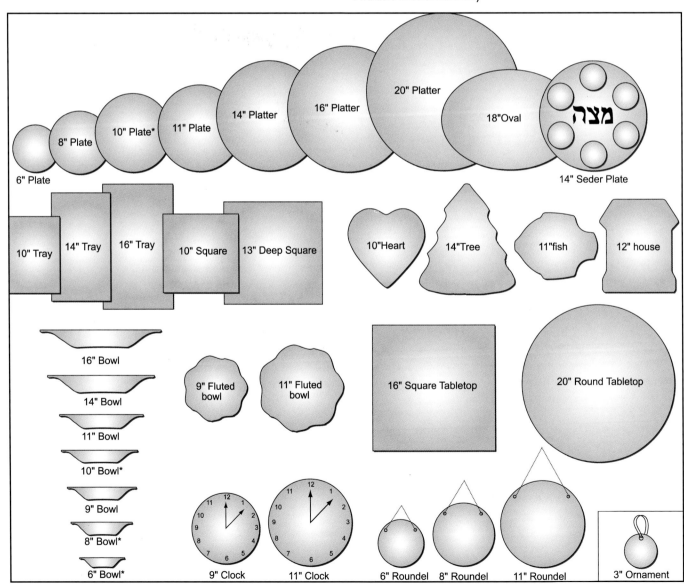

6" Plate   8" Plate   10" Plate*   11" Plate   14" Platter   16" Platter   20" Platter   18"Oval   מצה   14" Seder Plate

10" Tray   14" Tray   16" Tray   10" Square   13" Deep Square   10"Heart   14"Tree   11"fish   12" house

16" Bowl   14" Bowl   11" Bowl   10" Bowl*   9" Bowl   8" Bowl*   6" Bowl*   9" Fluted bowl   11" Fluted bowl   16" Square Tabletop   20" Round Tabletop

9" Clock   11" Clock   6" Roundel   8" Roundel   11" Roundel   3" Ornament

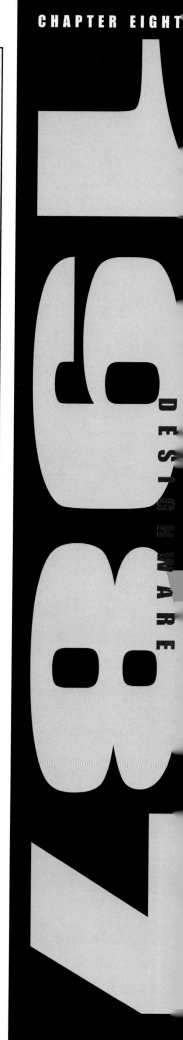

Checkerboard Animals were the first patterns I created when I started Peggy Karr Glass. Their inspiration actually came from two sources. When I first began to fuse glass my work was very contemporary. I had a hard time selling it at local craft fairs. At one in particular I sat next to a woman who had decorated ceramic jars with pigs, cows, and roosters. The people were lined up to purchase her pots. The second influence was my sister Ginny, who had decorated her kitchen with county animals and kept asking me to make her some plates. I really wanted to make a living at my craft so I figured if that's what they want, that's what I'll make. I chose the checkerboard as the format for my animals because I felt it helped make the animals cross over into other styles besides country. They were a perfect blend, country charm with a little hint of contemporary polish.

In total there were seventy-eight different animal designs, not counting color choices. Some of them had several different choices, like the cat that could be had as white, black, or grey, or the Butterfly fish that could be had in eight tropical colors. The very first design was the cow, shown above, which was the last one to be retired in 2000. Most of the others were retired by 1993. The Santa, Crab, Scotty, Buffalo, Loon, Horse, Tuxedo Cat, Lobster, Pig, Cow, Rooster, and Flamingo were still available in 1996 and included the new rectangular trays and 16" plate; but, all except the cow were retired in 1997.

All animals came in the 8", 11", 14", and 20" plates. Some animals were never made as a 20" plate, not because it wasn't available but because no one ever ordered it. On several occasions we tried to make bowls; but, for the most part when we fired them, the animals would get distorted when the glass stretched into the mold. In order to keep everyone happy we made plain checkerboard bowls and 6" plates without the animals as well as all the other sizes. If you think seventy-eight different animals is crazy, they came in an endless array of checkerboard color combinations. The most popular was black & white, of course, but there was also blue & white, red & white, red & green for Christmas, black & red, and the list goes on. There were twelve main color combinations. If you do the math it comes out to over 4,000 possibilities. When we enameled them we would often make a few extra because it didn't make sense to make only one. When we retired all the animals we had accumulated over $35,000 worth of one of these and two of those. It took us forever to finally sell all of them at our second sales. I designed all the Checkerboard Animals, except for five of the old cars that were done by Pat Provost.

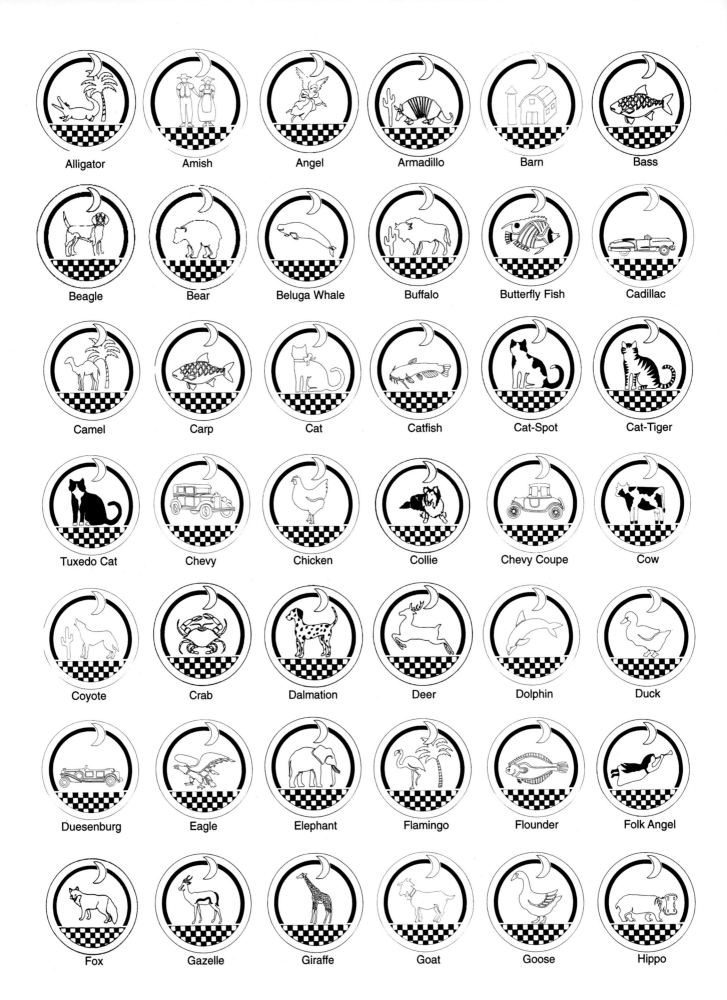

Alligator
Amish
Angel
Armadillo
Barn
Bass

Beagle
Bear
Beluga Whale
Buffalo
Butterfly Fish
Cadillac

Camel
Carp
Cat
Catfish
Cat-Spot
Cat-Tiger

Tuxedo Cat
Chevy
Chicken
Collie
Chevy Coupe
Cow

Coyote
Crab
Dalmation
Deer
Dolphin
Duck

Duesenburg
Eagle
Elephant
Flamingo
Flounder
Folk Angel

Fox
Gazelle
Giraffe
Goat
Goose
Hippo

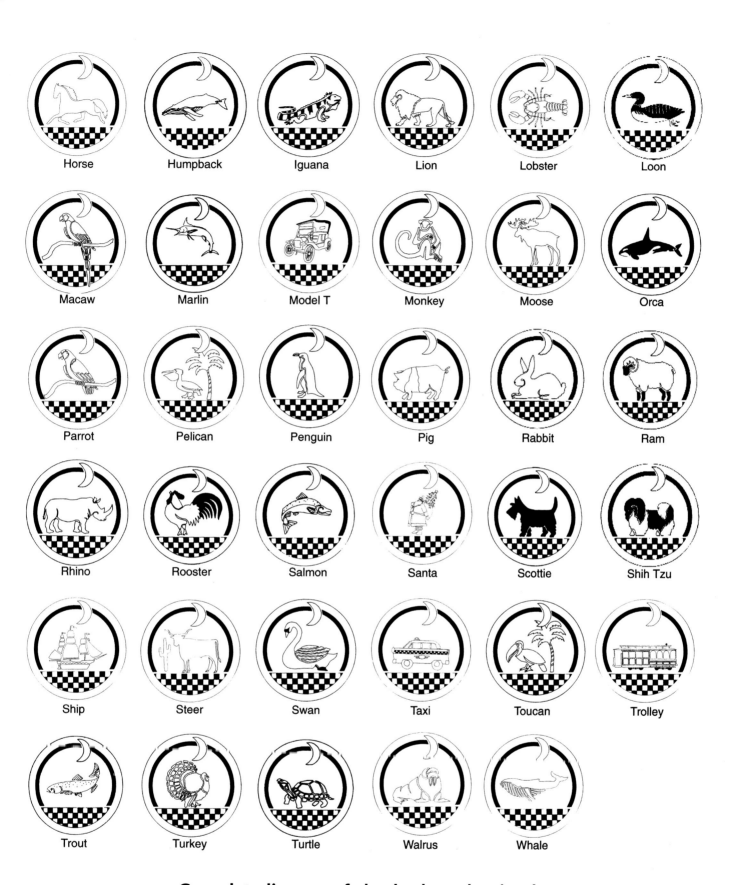

| Horse | Humpback | Iguana | Lion | Lobster | Loon |

| Macaw | Marlin | Model T | Monkey | Moose | Orca |

| Parrot | Pelican | Penguin | Pig | Rabbit | Ram |

| Rhino | Rooster | Salmon | Santa | Scottie | Shih Tzu |

| Ship | Steer | Swan | Taxi | Toucan | Trolley |

| Trout | Turkey | Turtle | Walrus | Whale |

## Complete line up of checkerboard animals

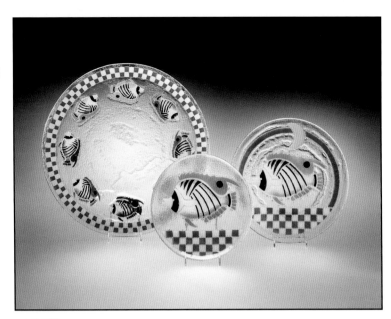

Checkerboard
Butterfly fish

Checkerboard Santa

Examples of checkerboard
color choices

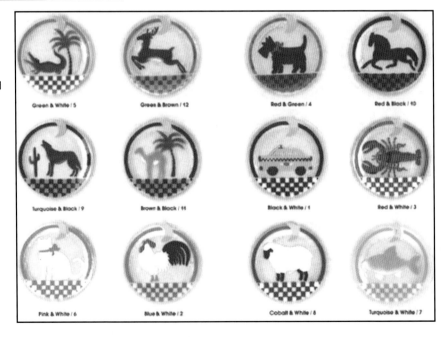

Green & White / 5    Green & Brown / 12    Red & Green / 4    Red & Black / 10

Turquoise & Black / 9    Brown & Black / 11    Black & White / 1    Red & White / 3

Pink & White / 6    Blue & White / 2    Cobalt & White / 8    Turquoise & White / 7

## CHECKERBOARD VEGGIES

By: Peggy Karr. Introduced-1988. Retired-2000. Availability-Common. Sizes: 6, 8, 11, 14, 16, 20 Inch Plates; 9, 11, 14, 16 Inch Bowls; 10, 14 Inch Trays; 13 Inch Square; 9 Inch Clock; 20 Inch Table. Comments: Vegetables was my first departure from the Checkerboard Animals. I was still in love with the checkerboard theme and it had become my trademark. I put the main design on the fourteen-inch and larger plates and then broke out all the different singular vegetables into the smaller sizes. There were originally twelve different patterns: Asparagus, Bean Pod, Carrot, Corn, Eggplant, Mushroom, Onion, Pepper, Radish, Tomato, Artichoke, and Chili Pepper. In 1996 we reduced the selection down to eight of the best selling vegetables. The Checkerboards came in several different color combinations, the most popular being black/white followed by blue/white, cobalt/white, green/white, and red/white.

## CHECKERBOARD FRUIT

By: Peggy Karr. Introduced-1988. Retired-2000. Availability-Common. Sizes: 6, 8, 11, 14, 16, 20 Inch Plates; 9, 11, 14, 16 Inch Bowls; 10, 14 Inch Trays; 13 Inch Square; 9 Inch Clock; 20 Inch Table. Comments: Fruit was my second departure from the Checkerboard Animals. The Fruit followed the same format as the Vegetables. There were originally twelve different fruits on the smaller plates: Apple, Banana, Blueberry, Cherry, Grape, Orange, Pear, Pineapple, Plum, Raspberry, Strawberry, and Watermelon. In 1996 we reduced the selection down to the eight best selling fruit. The Checkerboards came in several different combinations, the most popular being black/white, followed by blue/white, cobalt/white, green/white, and red/white.

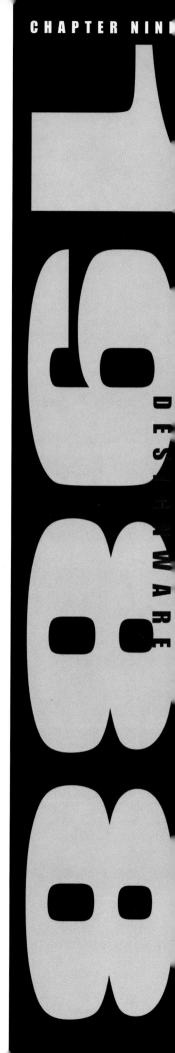

## CHAPTER NINE

# INDIVIDUAL CHECKERBOARD VEGGIES

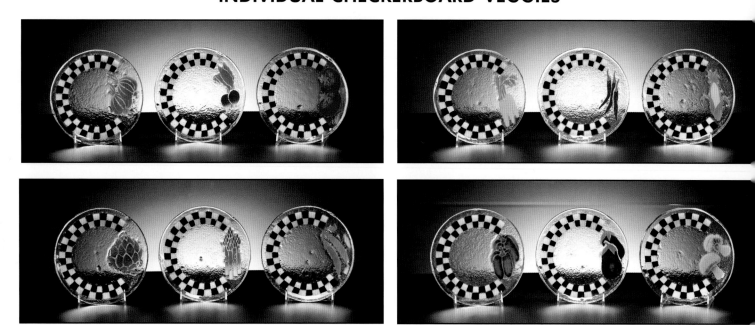

# INDIVIDUAL CHECKERBOARD FRUIT

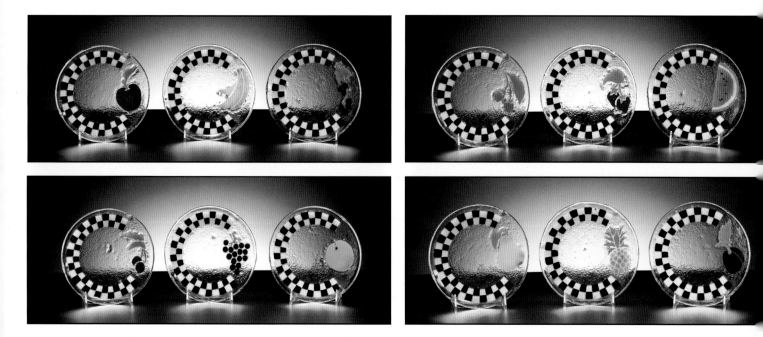

## CHAPTER TEN

# FLORAL

By: Peggy Karr. Introduced-1989. Retired-1989. Availability-Rare. Sizes: 6, 8, 11, 14 Inch Plates; 9, 11, 14 Inch Bowls. Comments: This was one of my first breaks from the Checkerboard theme. There were six different flowers: Tulip, Iris, Lily, Mum, Black-eyed Susan, and Poppy. All of the flowers were retired after a year, except the Iris. There is something about the dark blue Iris that everyone loves.

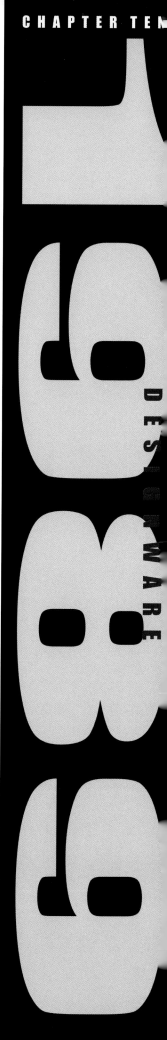

# OLD TIMEY

By: Peggy Karr. Introduced-1989. Retired-1992. Availability-Rare. Sizes: 6, 8, 14 Inch Plates. Comments: My father had an antique "Gibson Girl" book which contained old Victorian illustrations I used as my inspiration for these plates. There was a Golf Man, Golf Woman, Romance, Bicycle for Two, Tennis Man, Tennis Woman and a Beach Scene. There were also a few eight inch plates which were an adaptation from the backgrounds of the main plates, including a Golf Course, Beach Scene, and Grassy Field.

## BOW VINE

By: Peggy Karr. Introduced-1989. Retired-1993. Availability-Rare. Sizes: 6, 8, 11, 14, 20 Inch Plates; 9, 11, 14 Inch Bowls; 20 Inch Table. Comments: After I named the pattern Bow Vine I realized people thought it was bovine, referring to cattle. I should have named it Vines and Bows. Unfortunately it was too late to change the name in the catalog. The pattern came in five different styles: Grapes, Lilacs, Morning Glories, and Posies. They all had the same vine and bow border along the top edge of the plate.

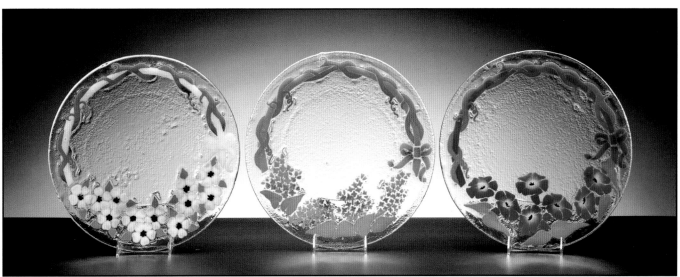

# KAY'S KRAZY KIDS

By: Mary Kay Mickiewicz. Introduced-1989. Retired-1989. Availability-Rare.
Sizes: 8, 9, 11, 14, 20 Inch Plates. Comments: Mary Kay kept doodling those
"Kids" on everything at the studio. She would cut them out and hang them
everywhere, so one day I asked her to make a plate with them and everyone
loved it. The smaller sizes had four different "Kids".

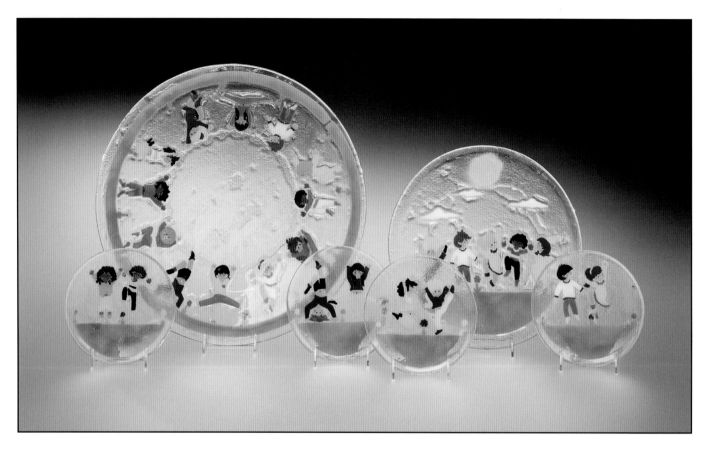

# SAILING

By Carol Haskell. Introduced-1989. Retired-1989. Availability-Rare.
Sizes: 8, 14 Inch Plates. Comments: Carol designed our first sailboat.
We have actually designed five different sailboat plates through the
years but this one was never photographed and only existed as a line
drawing in my 1989 catalog.

# ST. PATRICK'S DAY

By: Chris Krupinski. Introduced-1989. Retired-1989. Availability-Rare.
Sizes: 8, 14 Inch Plates. Comments: Chris only worked for me for a
short time and her St. Patrick's Day was never photographed. It only
existed as a line drawing in my second catalog. We revisited the
"Irish" in 1999 and designed a shamrock plate that is still in the line
today.

## CHAPTER ELEVEN

## VICTORIAN WREATH

By: Peggy Karr. Introduced-1990. Retired-1995. Availability-Limited. Sizes: 6, 8, 11, 14, 16, 20 Inch Plates; 9, 11, 14, 16 Inch Bowls; 9 Inch Clock; 20 Inch Table. Comments: Victorian Wreath was part of my wreath series, consisting of three different designs, including Country Wreath and Winter Wreath. The smaller sizes first had a single flower from the main design, they were a pink Rose, a white Petunia, blue Forget-me-nots, and purple Pansies. In 1993 we retired the single flower plates and reduced the main design to fit on the smaller sizes.

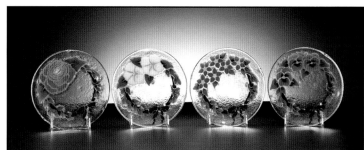

## CACTUS

By: Peggy Karr. Introduced-1990. Retired-1993. Availability-Limited. Sizes: 6, 8, 11, 14, 20 Inch Plates; 9, 11, 14 Inch Bowls; 20 Inch Table. Comments: I was still working with the checker-board theme and used the same format as the Fruit and Vegetable patterns. There were four different cactus on the smaller sizes: Pear cactus, tall Saguaro cactus, squatty Peyote cactus, and a round Barrel cactus.

## SPRING-GARDEN

By: Peggy Karr. Introduced-1990. Retired-2000. Availability-Common. Sizes: 6, 8, 11, 14, 16, 20 Inch Plates; 9, 11, 14, 16 Inch Bowls; 9, 11 Inch Fluted Bowls; 10, 14 Inch Trays; 13 Inch Square; 10 Inch Heart; 16, 20 Inch Tables; 9 Inch Clock; 6, 8, 11 Inch Roundels. Comments: Spring Garden was a very popular pattern. As with most of our early designs, the small plates showed only part of the larger design. As we were cutting all the stencils by hand, it was difficult to get very much detail in the smaller plates. As we became more proficient, we were able to shrink the main design to fit in the smaller plates and make them more desirable. The original four smaller designs were Daffodil, Crocus, Lily of the Valley, and Tulip.

## SOUTH WEST

By: Suzy Arvidson. Introduced-1990. Retired-1993. Availability-Rare. Sizes: 6, 8, 11, 14, 20 Inch Plates; 9, 11, 14 Inch Bowls; 20 Inch Table. Comments: South West was one of the first in a series of natural environment designs. The smaller sizes contained only a part of the main pattern, namely a lizard, coyote, snake, and hawk with cactus as the connecting theme. This was one of the first pieces that required delicate shading. It was needed in order to correctly portray the mountains in the background.

## COWBOY, INDIAN & SUNSET

By: Pat N. Provost. Introduced-1990. Retired-1990. Availability-Rare. Sizes: 8, 14 Inch Plates. Comments: The Cowboy, Indian, and eight inch Sunset plates were a set designed by Pat. She left the company to pursue her own fused glass interests at the end of 1990.

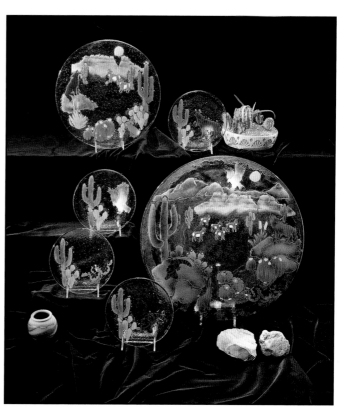

## TROPICAL FISH

By: Suzy Arvidson. Introduced-1990. Retired-1996. Availability-Common. Sizes: 6, 8, 11, 14, 16, 20 Inch Plates; 9, 11, 14, 16 Inch Bowls; 10, 14 Inch Trays; 9 Inch Clock; 6, 8, 11 Inch Roundels; 16, 20 Inch Tables. Comments: The Tropical Fish design was part of the natural environment series. The four smaller fish plates were the blue Queen Angel, the red and white Clown fish, the little multicolored Wrasse, and the elegant yellow and black French Angel Fish. We later retired all the single fish designs and simply shrank the main design to fit on the smaller sizes.

# SOLAR SYSTEM

By: Peggy Karr. Introduced-1990. Retired-1993. Availability-Rare. Sizes: 6, 8, 11, 14, 20 Inch Plates; 9, 11, 14 Inch Bowls; 20 Inch Table. Comments: My father was an amateur astronomer, so as a child I spent a lot of time looking through a telescope. There were four different patterns on the smaller sizes which all used the sun as the connecting theme with various other planets. Later we replaced the four different plates with a reduced version of the full design.

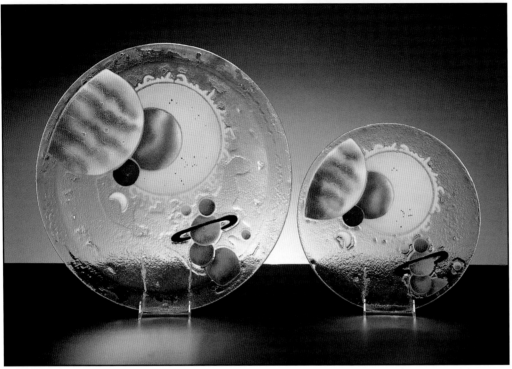

# SAILBOAT

By: Mary Ellen Whiteley. Introduced-1990. Retired-1993. Availability-Rare. Sizes: 8, 14 Inch Plate. Comments: Sailboat was Mary Ellen's only design. It was the second in the line of five sailboats we eventually produced.

# HUMMINGBIRD

By: Peggy Karr. Introduced-1990. Retired-1993. Availability-Rare. Sizes: 14 Inch Plates. Comments: My husband's grandmother, Lela Seitz, loved Hummingbirds, so I designed this plate for her 80th birthday.

## BALLOON, BIPLANE & PIPER CUB

By: Peggy Karr. Introduced-1990. Retired-1992. Availability-Rare.
Sizes: 14 Inch Plate. Comments: I was a big hot air balloon enthusiast.
I dated a man who owned one, so I "went aloft" often. It is a great
experience, which I highly recommend. He would take the balloon to
air shows where I was exposed to old airplanes and decided to add a
biplane and Piper Cub to the plate set.

## WINTER WREATH

By: Peggy Karr. Introduced-1990. Retired-1997. Availability-
Average. Sizes: 6, 8, 11, 14, 16, 20 Inch Plates; 9, 11, 14, 16
Inch Bowls; 10, 14 Inch Trays; 6, 8, 11 Inch Roundels; 20 Inch
Table. Comments: Winter Wreath was the most popular of
the three wreath designs and was the last to be retired. The
four smaller sizes were Holly, Mistletoe, Pinecone, and
Poinsettia. In 1993 we retired the four smaller designs and
reduced the fourteen-inch design to fit on the smaller sizes.

## CHAPTER TWELVE

## SUMMER GARDEN

By: Peggy Karr. Introduced-1991. Retired-1997. Availability-Common. Sizes: 6, 8, 11, 14, 16, 20 Inch Plates; 9, 11, 14, 16 Inch Bowls; 10, 14 Inch Trays; 9 Inch Clock; 20 Inch Table. Comments: The Spring Garden plate had done so well I decided to do a "Summer" version. Originally, the smaller sizes were white and pink Lilies, yellow Buttercups, purple Anemones, and little Bluebells. In 1993 we discontinued the separate flowers and reduced the main design to fit, so there was only one choice, which sold much better than the single flowers.

## COUNTRY WREATH

By: Peggy Karr. Introduced-1991. Retired-1993. Availability-Rare. Sizes: 6, 8, 11, 14, 20 Inch Plates; 9, 11, 14 Inch Bowls; 20 Inch Table. Comments: Country Wreath was the first of the wreath series to be retired; however, it was my favorite. I loved the big white daisies. The smaller sizes contained the white Daisy, pink Thistle, yellow Primrose, and purple Violets.

## HERBS

By: Donna A. Orsini. Introduced-1991. Retired-1995. Availability-Limited. Sizes: 6, 8, 11, 14, 16, 20 Inch Plates; 9, 11, 14, 16 Inch Bowls; 8, 9, 11 Inch Clocks; 20 Inch Table. Comments: Herbs was one of the first designs to include delicate details, making it very difficult to cut the stencils. This design had eight choices in the smaller sizes including Sage, Thyme, Dill, Chives, Rosemary, Mint, Basil, and Oregano. The plates all had the names of the herbs enameled in black on each plate. When we added clocks to the line, one of the first patterns was "Thyme". We loved the play on words.

## IVY

By: Mary Kay Mickiewicz. Introduced-1991. Retired-1995. Availability-Average. Sizes: 6, 8, 11, 14, 16, 20 Inch Plates; 9, 11, 14, 16 Inch Bowls; 10, 14 Inch Trays; 9 Inch Clock; 20 Inch Table. Comments: Mary Kay designed the first Ivy plate. It was a classic design that did very well in its time.

## MARSH

By: Diane C. Johnston. Introduced-1991. Retired-1997. Availability-Rare. Sizes: 6, 8, 11, 14, 16, 20 Inch Plates; 9, 11, 14, 16 Inch Bowls; 10, 14 Inch Trays; 9 Inch Clock; 20 Inch Table. Comments: The Marsh was another natural environment design. There were several different choices in a variety of sizes. There was a Turtle, Dragonfly, Frog, or Heron in the smaller sizes and there were two different 14 inch platters, Marsh Heron and Marsh Dragonfly. The 20-inch platter contained all of the elements.

## RACCOONS

By: Darren Bizzell. Introduced-1991. Retired-1993. Availability-Rare. Sizes: 8, 14 Inch Plates; 9 Inch Clock. Comments: Darren was a long time employee who worked in both the decorating and shipping departments. He was very artistic but never really got involved designing plates. Raccoons was his only design.

## FROGS

By: Diane C. Johnston. Introduced-1991. Retired-1993. Availability-Rare. Sizes: 8, 14 Inch Plates; 9 Inch Clock. Comments: A lot of people collected frogs. We had one client who was a huge collector and had us produce a custom frog every year. He gave them away at the holidays to all his friends and clients. We figured if frogs were that popular we should have one in the line.

## KITTENS

By: Peggy Karr. Introduced-1991. Retired-1993. Availability-Rare. Sizes: 8, 14 Inch Plates; 8, 9 Inch Clocks. Comments: The Kittens were cute but I lost control over the number of choices. There were eight different Kittens in all, the most popular being Black, followed by the Tabby. Then there was White, Grey, Spotted, Orange, Calico, and Siamese. Because all the stencils were cut by hand, we decided to use the same stencils for all the different Kittens so we didn't have to cut another set. That meant that there were a million different instructions on each stencil to tell the decorator how to color each Kitten.

## INDIAN STAG

By: David T. Switzer. Introduced-1991. Retired-1995. Availability-Rare. Sizes: 6, 8, 11, 14, 20 Inch Plates; 9, 11, 14 Inch Bowls; 8, 11 Inch Clocks; 20 Inch Table. Comments: David adapted this design from a collection of old Indian designs in a book. He was very inventive in his ability to achieve a "leather" effect through color and shading.

## BEACH UMBRELLA

By: David T. Switzer. Introduced-1991. Retired-1993. Availability-Rare. Sizes: 8, 14 Inch Plates. Comments: Originally David created a custom plate with beach umbrellas as an adaptation from a painting by a private artist. We all thought it looked so good I asked David to create his own version of "Beach Umbrellas".

## SHELLS

By: Donna A. Orsini. Introduced-1991. Retired-1993. Availability-Rare. Sizes: 8, 14 Inch Plates; 9, 11 Inch Clocks; 6, 8, 11 Inch Roundels. Comments: Shells was Donna's first pattern. The shading was so intricate that only a few of the best decorators could properly do the design.

## OCEAN FROLIC

By: Diane C. Johnston. Introduced-1991. Retired-1993. Availability-Rare. Sizes: 8, 14 Inch Plates; 8 Inch Clock. Comments: The graphic treatment of the water in Ocean Frolic was a great effect. It was reminiscent of some of the work Diane had done in her ceramic tile days.

## CAROUSEL

By: Suzy K. Arvidson. Introduced-1991. Retired-1995. Availability-Rare. Sizes: 6, 8, 11, 14, 20 Inch Plates; 9, 11 Inch Bowls; 9 Inch Clock; 20 Inch Table. Comments: Suzy had a lot of fun designing these plates. She especially loved carousel animals, so she had a difficult time deciding which animals to use. She finally settled on a Blue Horse, White Unicorn, Lion, and Tiger that could be had separately. There were six animals on the 20 inch platter, including a Zebra and an Elk. The design was first called Merry-Go-Round and later shortened to Carousel.

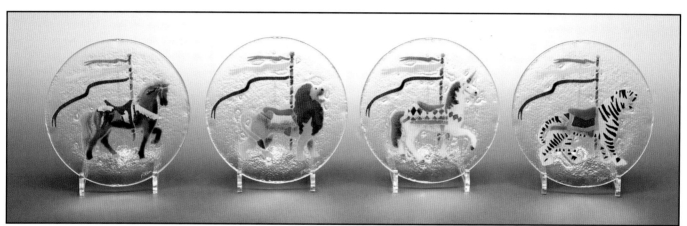

## CANDY

By: Suzy K. Arvidson. Introduced-1991. Retired-1997. Availability-Average. Sizes: 6, 8, 11, 14, 16, 20 Inch Plates; 9, 11, 14, 16 Inch Bowls; 10, 14 Inch Trays; 13 Inch Square; 20 Inch Table. Comments: Everyone loved Candy. It brought back memories of all those special red and white peppermint candy canes you got at Christmas time. It would still be in the line except it had a terrible bubble problem and we often had to make three plates to get two good ones, so we ultimately had to retire the design.

## NURSERY

By: Salli-Ann Mullen. Introduced-1991. Retired-1993. Availability-Rare. Sizes: 8, 11, 14 Inch Plates; 8, 9, 11 Inch Clocks. Comments: Salli-Ann loved being a Grandma and designed these plates based on the nursery rhymes she loved to read to her grandchildren. There was Jack & Jill, Little Boy Blue, Jack be Nimble, Humpty Dumpty, Little Miss Muffet, and Little Bo Peep. Each character came in only one size and they ranged from eight to fourteen inches. A sleeping baby, in several different colors and two sizes, was added to the line in 1992.

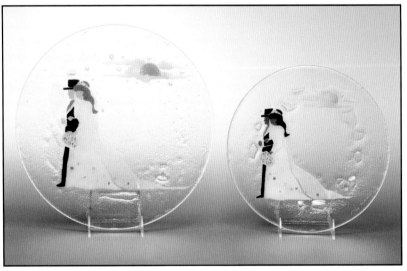

## WEDDING

By: Mary Kay Mickiewicz. Introduced-1991. Retired-1997. Availability-Average. Sizes: 8, 11, 14 Inch Plates. Comments: Mary Kay seemed to always have a wedding to attend, so she designed the Wedding plate to be used as gifts. Donna updated the design in 1998, but the ornament version is still in the line today.

## SWANS

By: Mary Kay Mickiewicz. Introduced-1991. Retired-1992. Availability-Rare. Sizes: 6, 8, 11, 14, 20 Inch Plates; 9, 11, 14 Inch Bowls. Comments: In addition to weddings, Mary Kay was also invited to many showers. Swans became the perfect gift for all of her special occasions and a companion piece for the Wedding design. We figured if they were good enough for us to give as gifts we should offer them in the catalog.

## CHAPTER THIRTEEN

### BEARDED IRIS

By: Vanessa Barresse. Introduced-1992. Retired-1993. Availability-Rare. Sizes: 6, 8, 11, 14 Inch Plates; 9, 11, 14 Inch Bowls. Comments: Vanessa had been with the company for three years and wanted to try her hand at designing. The Bearded Iris was her only design.

### LONG STEMMED TULIPS

By: Salli-Ann Mullen. Introduced-1992. Retired-1993. Availability-Rare. Sizes: 6, 8, 11, 14, 20 Inch Plates; 9, 11, 14 Inch Bowls; 20 Inch Table Comments: Salli-Ann was an avid gardener and loved tulips. She brought some from her garden as reference when she designed the plate.

### MUSHROOMS

By: Beth Ziolkowski. Introduced-1992. Retired-1993. Availability-Rare. Sizes: 6, 8, 11, 14, 20 Inch Plates; 9, 11, 14 Inch Bowls; 20 Inch Table. Comments: Toadstools was Beth's first design. The smaller sizes contained part of the main pattern and were identified by the main color of the mushroom: blue, green, orange, and red.

### SONGBIRDS

By: David Switzer. Introduced-1992. Retired-1993. Availability-Rare. Sizes: 6, 8, 11, 14, 20 Inch Plates; 9, 11, 14 Inch Bowls; 16, 20 Inch Tables; 8, 9, 11 Inch Clocks. Comments: Songbirds was a good design that drove customer service and shipping crazy. There were so many variations loosely based on the seasons that no one could keep them straight. The cutest was the six-inch plate, which had a little birds nest as the design.

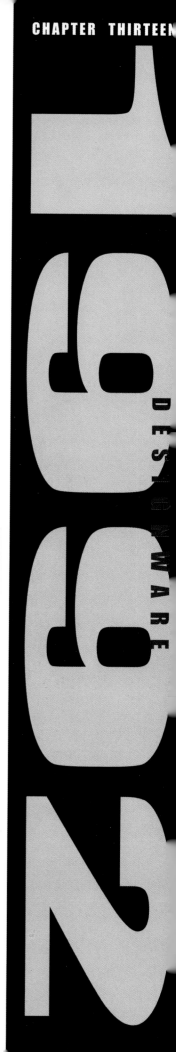

## CUBES

By: Peggy Karr. Introduced-1992. Retired-1993. Availability-Rare.
Sizes: 6, 8, 11, 14, 20 Inch Plates; 9, 11, 14 Inch Bowls; 20 Inch Table.
Comments: Cubes was a design that was inspired by my geometric
days back in 1986 when I first started to use enamels. I found an old
drawing and decided to give it a try. As it was very out of character
for Peggy Karr Glass, it wasn't a great seller; but, I revisit this look in
2004. Cubes was available in various color choices shown in the
photograph.

## BAND OF ELEPHANTS

By: Peggy Karr. Introduced-1992. Retired-1993. Availability-Rare.
Sizes: 6, 8, 11, 14, 20 Inch Plates; 9, 11, 14 Inch Bowls; 20 Inch Table.
Comments: I had originally intended to do several different animal
boarders, but the lack of success of Elephants caused me to give up
the idea.

## ROSES (1992)

By: Peggy Karr. Introduced-1992. Retired-1993. Availability-Rare.
Sizes: 6, 8, 11, 14, 20 Inch Plates; 9, 11, 14 Inch Bowls; 20 Inch Table.
Comments: I thought Roses would be a "slam-dunk", especially at
Valentines Day, but this design never took off. I guess people like to
buy real roses more than roses on a plate.

## AFRICAN SILHOUETTE

By: Jeff Wallace. Introduced-1992. Retired-1993. Availability-Rare.
Sizes: 8, 11, 14 Inch Plates. Comments: Jeff worked in the decorating
department for many years before ultimately becoming one of the
supervisors. He created African Silhouette and used images of an
elephant, a gazelle, a giraffe, and a lion on the smaller plates. (Also
shown here, Indian Stag 1991)

## HUNT

By: David T. Switzer. Introduced-1992. Retired-1995. Availability-
Rare. Sizes: 6, 8, 11, 14, 16, 20 Inch Plates; 9, 11, 14 Inch Bowls; 16,
20 Inch Tables; 9, 11 Inch Clocks. Comments: David had a lot of fun
hiding the little fox behind the wall. Originally it was called "Out-
foxed", but we changed the name to "Hunt". The four different
smaller plates were Fox, Horses, Hounds, and Jumper. In 1993 we
retired all the different choices and redesigned one pattern for the
smaller sizes.

## GOLF

By: Peggy Karr. Introduced-1992. Retired-1997. Availability-Average. Sizes: 6, 8, 11, 14, 16, 20 Inch Plates; 10, 14 Inch Trays; 13 Inch Square; 20 Inch Table; 8, 9 Clocks; 6, 8, 11 Inch Roundels. Comments: Everyone missed the golfers from the "Old Timey" series, so I decided to try a more contemporary approach to the sport. There were three different variations: Men, Women, and a simple Golf Green. There was a single golfer on the 8-inch, a twosome on the 14 inch, and a foursome on the 20 inch platter.

## BOUGH

By: Diane Johnston. Introduced-1992. Retired-1997. Availability-Average. Sizes: 6, 8, 11, 14, 16, 20 Inch Plates; 9, 11, 14, 16 Inch Bowls; 10, 14 Inch Trays; 20 Inch Table. Comments: Bough was our first attempt at a Christmas ornament plate. Diane used some of her favorite antique ornaments as reference.

# STARS

By: Donna Orsini DesJadon. Introduced-1992. Retired-2001. Availability-Numerous. Sizes: 6, 8, 11, 14, 16, 20 Inch Plates; 9, 11, 14, 16 Inch Bowls; 10, 14 Inch Trays; 13 Inch Square; 16, 20 Inch Tables; 8, 9, 11 Inch Clocks; 6, 8, 11 Inch Roundels. Comments: I asked Donna to do something festive with stars in the border. The plate she designed worked wonderfully for all sorts of celebrations and was an immediate success. It remained in the line for ten years. Stars was available in two other color ways. One was red, white and blue; the other was called Folk Stars and was burgundy, cream, and forest.

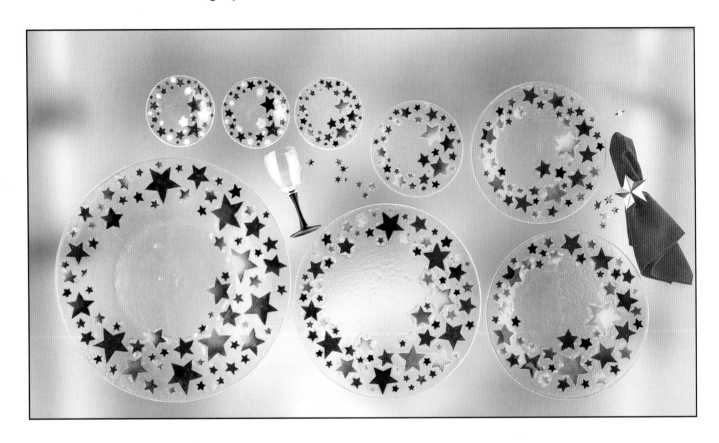

# MAMMY

By: Salli-Ann Mullen. Introduced-1992. Retired-1992. Availability-Rare. Sizes: 11, 14 Inch Plates; 9 Inch Clock. Comments: This design was requested by our African American customers. The only picture I could find was this one with both the Mammy and Rag Doll on a shelf in one of our booths. I wish we had saved more of the old plates, it didn't occur to us that they would be an important part of our history.

# RAG DOLL

By: Salli-Ann Mullen. Introduced-1992. Retired-1992. Availability-Rare. Sizes: 11, 14 Inch Plates. Comments: Salli-Ann was great at designing things for children. Since we retired her last children's theme plate we have never designed another.

## CHAPTER FOURTEEN

## IRIS

By: Peggy Karr. Introduced-1993.
Retired-NA. Availability-Numerous.
Sizes: 6, 8, 11, 14, 16, 20 Inch Plates;
9, 11, 14, 16 Inch Bowls; 9, 11 Inch
Fluted Bowls; 10, 14 Inch Trays; 13
Inch Square; 10 Inch Heart; 20 Inch
Table; 9 Inch Clock; 6, 8, 11 Inch
Roundels. Comments: Iris was part
of the earlier floral series. It is the
oldest pattern still in the catalog
today. It was first designed in 1989 as
a 14-inch plate; then, in 1993 it was
expanded into a full line. I can't
believe how well it sells after all
these years. I would love to redesign
it but everyone tells me "if it isn't
broken don't try to fix it".

## RABBITS

By: Suzy Arvidson. Introduced-
1993. Retired-2001. Availability-
Numerous. Sizes: 6, 8, 11, 14, 16,
20 Inch Plates; 9, 11, 14, 16 Inch
Bowls; 10, 14 Inch Trays; 13 Inch
Square; 10 Inch Heart; 20 Inch
Table; 9 Inch Clock; 6, 8, 11 Inch
Roundels. Comments: We really
needed something for spring and
what better than adorable white
bunnies frolicking in a vegetable
garden with multi-colored Sweet
Peas in the background. We
quickly discovered how popular
rabbits were as a theme.

## DOGWOOD

By: David Switzer. Introduced-1993. Retired-1995. Availability-Rare. Sizes: 6, 8, 11, 14, 16, 20 Inch
Plates; 9, 11, 14, 16 Inch Bowls; 9 Inch Clock; 20 Inch Table. Comments: David used the Dogwood
as a theme in several of his bird designs and decided to give it this "solo" treatment.

# HUMMINGBIRD & HIBISCUS

By: David Switzer. Introduced-1993. Retired-2000. Availability-Average. Sizes: 6, 8, 11, 14, 16, 20 Inch Plates; 9, 11, 14, 16 Inch Bowls; 9, 11 Inch Fluted Bowls; 10, 14 Inch Trays; 13 Inch Square; 10 Inch Heart; 20 Inch Table; 9 Inch Clock; 6, 8, 11 Inch Roundels. Comments: David redesigned my Hummingbird plate and gave it more detail and realism. The Hibiscus was beautiful and the little Ruby Throated Hummingbirds were adorable.

# SUN & MOON

By: Diane Johnston. Introduced-1993. Retired-1997. Availability-Limited. Sizes: 6, 8, 11, 14, 16, 20 Inch Plates; 9, 11, 14, 16 Inch Bowls; 10, 14 Inch Trays; 6, 8 Inch Roundel; 20 Inch Table; 9 Inch Clock. Comments: "Sun and Moon" is a popular theme. Diane gave both the sun and the moon faces a lot of character. When we came out with Colorware we tried gift boxing a set we called "Breakfast for Two - Sunny Side Up" which included Classic yellow plates with 8 inch sun plates as part of the set. We revisit this theme in 2002.

# SUNFLOWERS

By: Peggy Karr. Introduced-1993. Retired-1997. Availability-Limited. Sizes: 6, 8, 11, 14, 16, 20 Inch Plates; 9, 11, 14, 16 Inch Bowls; 10, 14 Inch Trays; 20 Inch Table; 9 Inch Clock; 20 Inch Table. Comments: Sunflowers have always been popular. I love the big droopy yellow flowers and had a good time designing the pattern. I discovered there are many different kinds of sunflowers, but my favorites are still the huge ones with the dark brown centers.

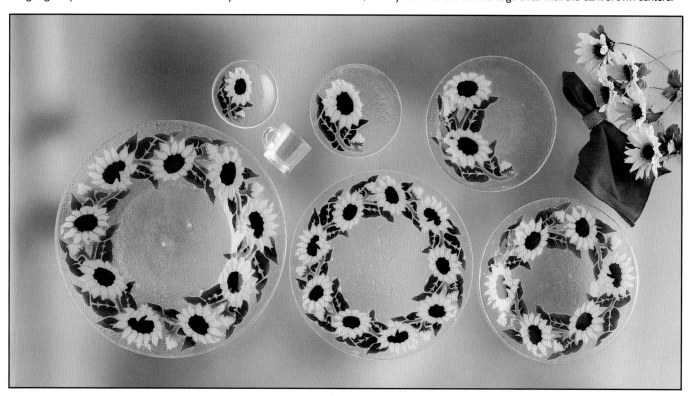

# OAK LEAVES

By: Peggy Karr. Introduced-1993. Retired-1995. Availability- Rare. Sizes: 6, 8, 11, 14, 16, 20 Inch Plates; 9, 11, 14, 16 Inch Bowls; 20 Inch Table.
Comments: Oak Leaves was my first attempt at a real autumn pattern. Autumn is a theme that the retailers always request but never sells very well.

# HARVEST GRAPE

By: Diane Johnston. Introduced-1993. Retire- 2001. Availability-Average. Sizes: 6, 8, 11, 14, 16, 20 Inch Plates; 9, 11, 14, 16 Inch Bowls; 10, 14 Inch Trays; 13 Inch Square; 20 Inch Table; 9 Inch Clock. Comments: Harvest Grape was very popular for a long time. In 1995 we bowed to customer pressure and changed the grapes from a cobalt blue to purple. Harvest Grape was also available in the Judaic line as Seder, Matzo, and Shabbat.

# HARVEST FRUIT

By: Diane Johnston. Introduced-1993. Retired-2000. Availability-Numerous. Sizes: 6, 8, 11, 14, 16, 20 Inch Plates; 9, 11, 14, 16 Inch Bowls; 10, 14 Inch Trays; 13 Inch Square; 16, 20 Inch Table; 9 Inch Clock; 6, 8 Inch Roundels. Comments: There were three patterns in the Harvest series, this being the most popular. It worked very well as an autumn piece and stayed in the line for a long time. Originally, the smaller pieces were parts of the main design and included pear, cherries, peach, and apple. Later Diane combined all the fruit onto one plate. It was also very popular as a clock.

# HARVEST VEGETABLE

By: Diane Johnston. Introduced-1993. Retired-1997. Availability-Average. Sizes: 6, 8, 11, 14, 16, 20 Inch Plates; 9, 11, 14, 16 Inch Bowls; 10, 14 Inch Trays; 9 Inch Clock; 20 Inch Table. Comments: Harvest Vegetable was the least popular of the Harvest series but it laid the groundwork for other vegetable patterns to follow.

# BOATING

By: Peggy Karr. Introduced-1993. Retired-1995. Availability-Rare. Sizes: 6, 8, 11, 14, 16, 20 Inch Plates; 9, 11, 14, 16 Inch Bowls; 20 Inch Table; 9 Inch Clock. Comments: Boating was our third attempt at doing a sailboat plate. It never captured the feeling I was looking for.

## SEA SHELLS (1993)

By: Suzy Arvidson. Introduced-1993. Retired-1997. Availability-Limited. Sizes: 6, 8, 11, 14, 16, 20 Inch Plates; 9, 11, 14, 16 Inch Bowls; 10, 14 Inch Trays; 20 Inch Table; 9 Inch Clock; 6, 8, 11 Inch Roundels. Comments: Suzy's approach to Sea Shells was bold and colorful. No pale pastels for her.

## METROPOLIS

By: Peggy Karr. Introduced-1993. Retired-1995. Availability-Rare. Sizes: 6, 8, 11, 14, 16, 20 Inch Plates; 9, 11, 14, 16 Inch Bowls; 20 Inch Table; 9 Inch Clock. Comments: Flying back from a business trip to Florida, in the plane I sketched out this plate inspired from the colors in Miami. Unfortunately, it was a little too out in left field for our customers at that time.

## COLUMNS

By: Peggy Karr. Introduced-1993. Retired-1995. Availability-Rare. Sizes: 6, 8, 11, 14, 20 Inch Plates; 9, 11, 14 Inch Bowls; 9 Inch Clock; 20 Inch Table. Comments: I was watching something on TV that gave me the idea for Columns. I made a quick sketch, which looked interesting, so I tried it as a plate. I liked it a lot; but, again, like Metropolis, it was a little to out in left field for our customers. (P.S. It's the pattern I use for my dinnerware at home.)

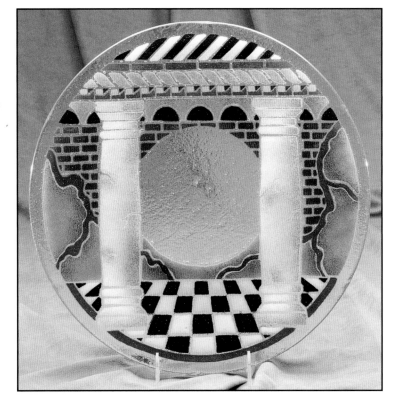

## RENAISSANCE

By: Donna Orsini DesJadon. Introduced-1993. Retired-1995. Availability-Rare. Sizes: 6, 8, 11, 14, 20 Inch Plates; 9, 11, 14 Inch Bowls; 9 Inch Clock. Comments: Donna got hooked on a book that had examples of Renaissance decoration and adapted one of the designs in the book to glass. It was available in two color ways, Pale and Bright, which was more popular.

## LEAF PATTERN

By: Beth Ziolkowski. Introduced-1993. Retired-1993. Availability-Rare. Sizes: 6, 8, 11, 14, 20 Inch Plates; 9, 11, 14 Inch Bowls; 20 Inch Table. Comments: This was a very unusual theme that resembled a kaleidoscope. It came in two color ways, blue and yellow, and only a few sizes.

## PINE WREATH

By: David Switzer. Introduced-1993. Retired-1995. Availability-Limited. Sizes: 6, 8, 11, 14, 16, 20 Inch Plates; 9, 11, 14, 16 Inch Bowls; 20 Inch Table. Comments: Pine Wreath was a well executed traditional theme that worked very well.

## XMAS HOLIDAY

By: Salli-Ann Mullen. Introduced-1993. Retired-1993. Availability-Rare.
Sizes: 6, 8, 11, 14, 20 Inch Plates; 9, 11, 14 Inch Bowls; 20 Inch Table.
Comments: The Carolers were a great idea that just didn't catch the
consumer's imagination.

## SKIING

By: Andy Barresse. Introduced-1993. Retired-1995. Availability-Rare.
Sizes: 6, 8, 11, 14, 20 Inch Plates; 9, 11, 14 Inch Bowls; 9 Inch Clock;
20 Inch Table. Comments: Andy loved all kinds of sports. He created
a whole series of clocks and ornaments with sporting equipment as
the theme.

## SLEIGH (1993)

By: Suzy Arvidson. Introduced-1993. Retired-1995. Availability-
Limited. Sizes: 6, 8, 11, 14, 16, 20 Inch Plates; 9, 11, 14, 16 Inch
Bowls; 6, 8, 11 Inch Roundels. Comments: Sleigh was our first
attempt at Santa and his reindeer. This rendition shows Santa riding
over a sleepy, snow-covered village.

## PANSIES

By: Donna Orsini DesJadon. Introduced-1994. Retired-NA. Availability-Numerous. Sizes: 6, 8, 11, 14, 16, 20 Inch Plates; 9, 11, 14, 16 Inch Bowls; 9, 11 Inch Fluted Bowls; 10, 14, 16 Inch Trays; 18 Inch Oval; 10, 13 Inch Square; 10 Inch Heart; 16, 20 Inch Tables; 9 Inch Clock; 6, 8, 11 Inch Roundels. Comments: Pansies has been a phenomenon for us. It's sales went thought the roof and it was our best selling plate for eight years straight. Every time we came up with a new shape we immediately added it to the Pansy collection. I think Pansies is one of the only patterns that has come in every size and shape we produce. Pansies were also available in the Judaic line as a Seder, Matzo, and Shabbat.

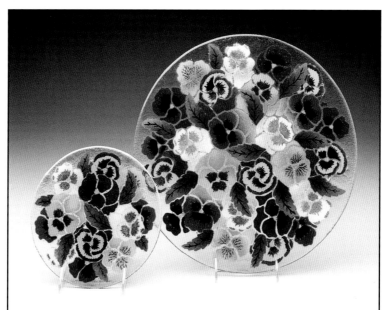

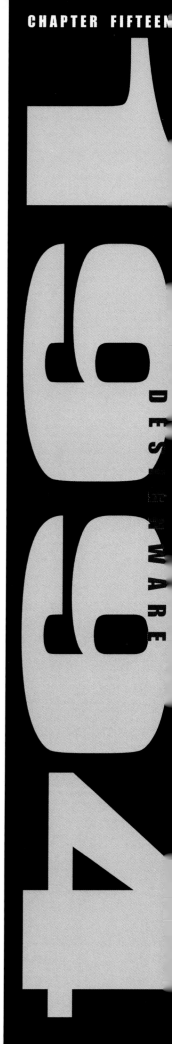

## CHAPTER FIFTEEN

## BIRDS ON DOGWOOD

By: David Switzer. Introduced-1994. Retired-1995. Availability-Rare. Sizes: 6, 8, 11, 14, 16, 20 Inch Plates; 9, 11, 14, 16 Inch Bowls; 20 Inch Table; 9 Inch Clock. Comments: Dave had designed plates with Birds and plates with Dogwood as a theme, so he decided to create a plate combining both elements.

## RAINBOW TROUT

By: David Switzer. Introduced-1994. Retired-1995. Availability-Rare. Sizes: 6, 8, 11, 14, 16, 20 Inch Plates; 9, 11, 14, 16 Inch Bowls; 10, 14 Inch Trays; 9 Clock; 6, 8, 11 Inch Roundels; 20 Inch Table. Comments: David enjoys designing wildlife. This is the first of two trout plates he has designed.

## WOODLAND

By: Peggy Karr. Introduced-1994. Retired-1994. Availability-Rare. Sizes: 6, 8, 11, 14, 16, 20 Inch Plates; 9, 11, 14, 16 Inch Bowls; 9 Inch Clock; 20 Inch Table. Comments: I should have followed my initial instinct and not finished Woodland, because it is my least favorite design. It was a graphic treatment of leaves with stripes in pale brown and cream colors.

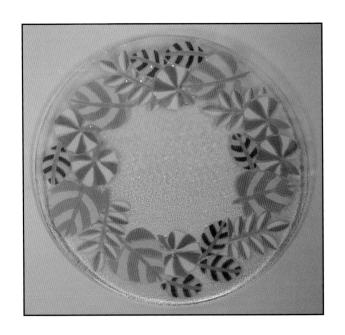

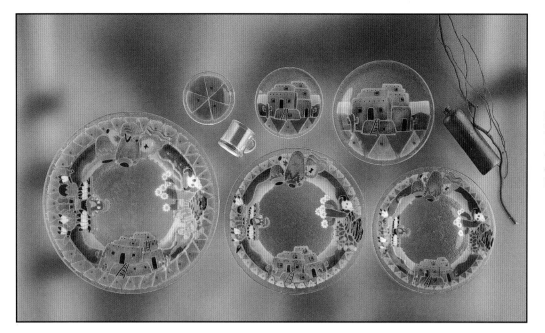

## PUEBLO

By: David Switzer. Introduced-1994. Retired-1995. Availability-Rare. Sizes: 6, 8, 11, 14, 16, 20 Inch Plates; 9, 11, 14, 16 Inch Bowls; 20 Inch Table. Comments: The striking pastel colors of the Southwest brought this plate to life.

## KOI POND

By: David Switzer. Introduced-1994. Retired-1995. Availability-Rare. Sizes: 6, 8, 11, 14, 16, 20 Inch Plates; 9, 11, 14, 16 Inch Bowls; 20 Inch Table; 9 Inch Clock. Comments: Koi Pond was a wonderful plate with the fish peeking out from under lilly pads. It had an Asian feel that was just beginning to appear in American home decor.

## HEARTLAND

By: Salli-Ann Mullen. Introduced-1994. Retired-1994. Availability-Rare. Sizes: 6, 8, 11, 14, 16, 20 Inch Plates; 9, 11, 14, 16 Inch Bowls; 9 Inch Clock; 20 Inch Table. Comments: Heartland had a Pennsylvania Dutch feel to the pattern. My sister loved it so much that she still has Heartland in her kitchen.

## ANGELS

By: Suzy Arvidson. Introduced-1994. Retired-1998. Availability-Common. Sizes: 6, 8, 11, 14, 16, 20 Inch Plates; 9, 11, 14, 16 Inch Bowls; 10, 14 Inch Trays; 13 Inch Square; 9 Inch Clock; 6, 8, 11 Inch Roundels; 20 Inch Table. Comments: Angels was extremely popular when it came out. The background color behind the filigree had to be just right so I created the color sage especially for the Angels.

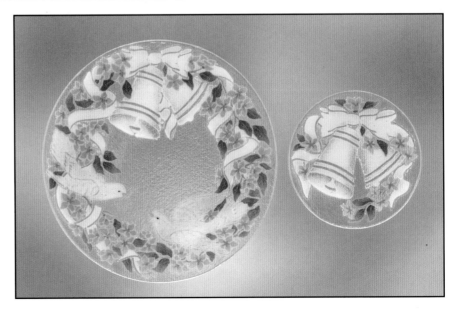

## HEARTS (1994)

By: Diane Johnston. Introduced-1994. Retired-2001. Availability-Numerous. Sizes: 8, 11, 14 Inch Plates; 9, 11, 14 Inch Bowls; 10, 14 Inch Trays; 10 Inch Heart; 13 Inch Square; 10 Inch Heart; 9 Inch Clock; 6, 8 Inch Roundels. Comments: This simplistic design sold very well, although no one at the studio cared for it. When we retired it customers complained, so we decided to redesign Hearts in 2003, making it very similar to this design.

## BELLS

By: Diane Johnston. Introduced-1994. Retired-1997. Availability-Rare. Sizes: 8, 14 Inch Plates. Comments: We had a wedding plate, but lots of people kept asking for an anniversary plate. Bells was in the line for a few years, but it was never as popular as either of the wedding plates. In the Judaic line it was called Hebrew Bells.

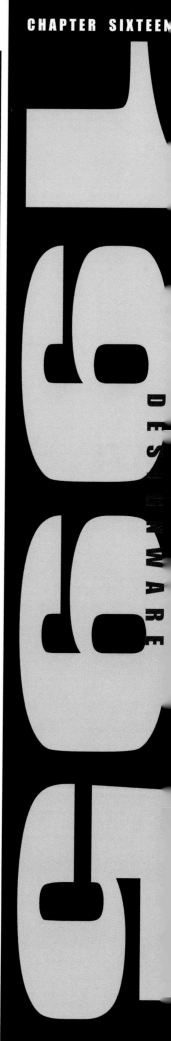

## CHAPTER SIXTEEN

## ANTIQUE FLORAL

By: Diane Johnston. Introduced-1995. Retired-2000. Availability-Common. Sizes: 6, 8, 11, 14, 16, 20 Inch Plates; 9, 11, 14, 16 Inch Bowls; 9, 11 Inch Fluted Bowls; 10, 14 Inch Trays; 13 Inch Square; 10 Inch Heart; 20 Inch Table; 9 Inch Clock. Comments: Diane's sense of color in this romantic floral wreath was excellent. She was able to capture the soft pastel flowers using multiple overlays in just the right colors.

## GARDEN CAT

By: Peggy Karr. Introduced-1995. Retired-2000. Availability-Common. Sizes: 6, 8, 11, 14, 16, 20 Inch Plates; 9, 11, 14, 16 Inch Bowls; 10, 14 Inch Trays; 13 Inch Square; 20 Inch Table; 9 Inch Clock; 6, 8, 11 Inch Roundels. Comments: Some plates are hard to design and others are easy. I saw this plate in my head and had it finished in no time with very few revisions. I had an orange tabby cat that used to lie around like the cat in the plate. I considered using my cat but I thought the tuxedo cat looked better.

## BIRDS ON HOLLY

By: David Switzer. Introduced-1995. Retired-1995.
Availability-Rare. Sizes: 6, 8, 11, 14, 16, 20 Inch Plates; 9,
11, 14, 16 Inch Bowls; 20 Inch Table. Comments: David
originally designed Songbirds in 1992. The cardinal was
the most popular bird, so he decided to try it again in this
winter theme.

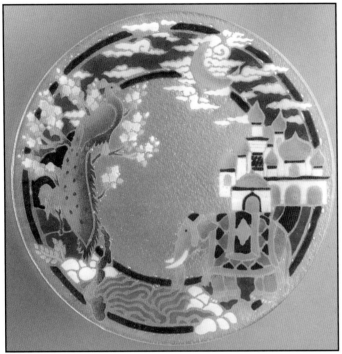

## MYSTIC NIGHT

By: Suzy Arvidson. Introduced-1995. Retired-1995.
Availability-Rare. Sizes: 6, 8, 11, 14, 16, 20 Inch
Plates; 9, 11, 14, 16 Inch Bowls; 20 Inch Table.
Comments: Suzy enjoyed designing environmental
imagery like this East Indian design.

## CORNUCOPIA

By: Diane Johnston. Introduced-1995.
Retired-1998. Availability-Rare. Sizes: 6,
8, 11, 14, 16, 20 Inch Plates; 9, 11, 14,
16 Inch Bowls; 10, 14 Inch Trays; 20 Inch
Table; 6, 8, 11 Inch Roundels. Comments: Cornucopia seemed like a natural
choice for the fall. The gourds and fruit
in the horn-shaped basket remind me of
Thanksgiving at my Grandmother's
house. She always decorated her table
with a Cornucopia.

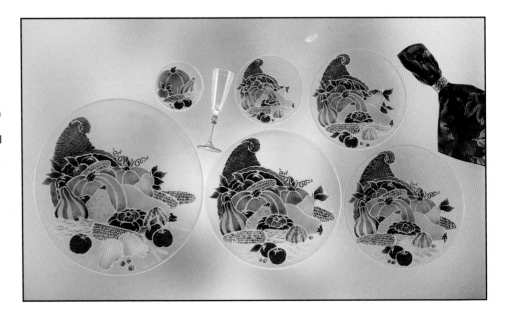

# HALLOWEEN

By: Salli-Ann Mullen. Introduced-1995. Retired-2001. Availability-Common. Sizes: 6, 8, 11, 14, 16 Inch Plates; 9, 11, 14 Inch Bowls; 10, 14 Inch Trays; 13 Inch Square; 6, 8, 11 Inch Roundels. Comments: Salli-Ann designed this adorable plate but we couldn't decide if it would sell. We gave it a try in a few sizes and what a big surprise. It became a huge success plus we added more sizes the following year.

## CHRISTMAS DAY

By: David Switzer. Introduced-1995.
Retired-1997. Availability-Rare. Sizes: 6,
8, 11, 14, 16, 20 Inch Plates; 9, 11, 14,
16 Inch Bowls; 10, 14 Inch Trays; 13 Inch
Square; 20 Inch Table; 6, 8, 11 Inch
Roundels. Comments: Christmas trees
have long been a strong theme for the
holidays. They can be seen in many
different mediums. David designed this
plate full of rich details such as the little
clock on the mantle and all the colorful
decorations on the tree.

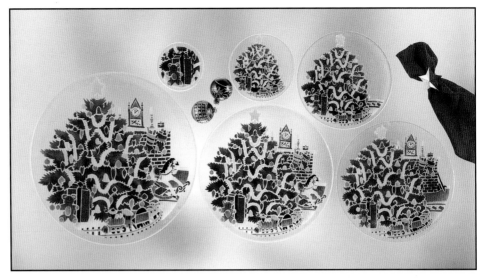

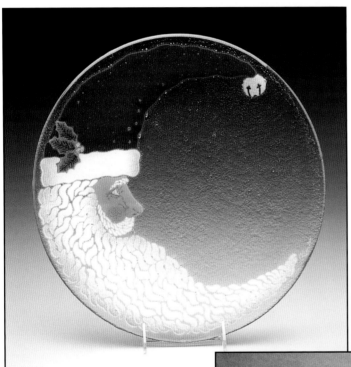

## ST. NICK

By: Donna Orsini DesJadon. Introduced-1995. Retired-NA.
Availability-Numerous. Sizes: 6, 8, 11, 14, 16, 20 Inch Plates; 9,
11, 14, 16 Inch Bowls; 10, 14 Inch Trays; 13 Inch Square; 20 Inch
Table; 6, 8, 11 Inch Roundels. Comments: St. Nick has been one
of our best selling Holiday plates for years. Donna did an
excellent job creating this whimsical version of Santa. The best
story related to this design is, when we came out with rectangles
and squares, of course we tried to put St. Nick in these shapes
because he was so popular. They are pictured here. We retired
them almost as soon as they were introduced because ... "You
can't fit a round shape into a square hole".

## CHAPTER SEVENTEEN

## MAGNOLIA

By: Donna Orsini DesJadon.
Introduced-1996. Retired-1999. Availability-Rare.
Sizes: 6, 8, 11, 14, 16, 20
Inch Plates; 9, 11, 14, 16
Inch Bowls; 9, 11 Inch
Fluted Bowls; 10, 14 Inch
Trays; 10 Inch Heart; 13
Inch Square; 20 Inch Table;
9 Inch Clock; 6, 8 Inch
Roundels. Comments:
Magnolia was a beautiful
plate. Donna did a lot of
research for this design
because we wanted to
create something that
would appeal to the South.

## LILACS

By: Diane Johnston. Introduced-1996. Retired-2001. Availability-Common. Sizes: 6, 8, 11, 14, 16, 20 Inch Plates; 9, 11, 14, 16 Inch Bowls; 9, 11 Inch Fluted Bowls; 10, 14 Inch Trays; 13 Inch Square; 10 Inch Heart; 20 Inch Table; 9 Inch Clock; 6, 8 Inch Roundels. Comments: This was one of the last plates made before we started to use the laser cutter for our stencils. Diane had to cut all those little petals by hand. Considering there were ten sizes, I don't know how she did it.

## EASTER BASKET

By: Salli-Ann Mullen. Introduced-1996. Retired-1997.
Availability-Rare. Sizes: 6, 8, 11, 14 Inch Plates; 9, 11, 14
Inch Bowls; 10, 14 Inch Trays; 13 Inch Square; 6, 8 Inch
Roundels. Comments: Salli-Ann had a cute sense of style
and had done such a good job with the Halloween plate
we thought she should try an Easter theme. The little
bunnies and chicks were adorable.

## MAGIC GARDEN

By: Beth Ellen. Introduced-1996. Retired-1997. Availability-Rare. Sizes: 6, 8, 11, 14, 16, 20 Inch Plates; 9, 11, 14,
16 Inch Bowls; 10, 14 Inch Trays; 20 Inch Table. Comments: The flowers and colors in Magic Garden were
great. Beth was just slightly ahead of, or behind if you
will, her time. I think she really captured the sixties. It
makes me remember "Laugh In" from TV.

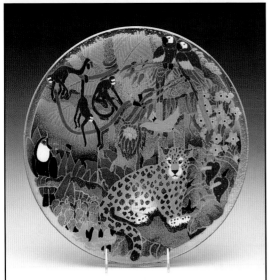

## RAINFOREST

By: Suzy Arvidson. Introduced-1996. Retired-1999. Availability-Rare. Sizes: 6, 8, 11, 14, 16, 20 Inch Plates; 9, 11, 14, 16 Inch Bowls; 10, 14 Inch Trays; 13 Inch Square; 20 Inch Table; 9 Inch Clock; 6, 8 Inch Roundels. Comments: Rainforest was another of Suzy's environmental themes and I think this was one of her best efforts. It came in several different sizes, using various parts of the main theme, jungle trees, as the common thread.

## HOMES

By: David Switzer. Introduced-1996. Retired-1998. Availability-Rare. Sizes: 14 Inch Plates. Comments: Homes was the first design where we began to work with silk-screening. All the fine detail was screened onto the underside of the top piece of glass with special black ink I designed. The remainder of the design was enameled the traditional way. When the two pieces of glass were fired together, the effect was like an illustration. There were three 14 inch plates in this series: Neighborhood, Oceanfront, and Farm.

## CHERUBS

By: Suzy Arvidson. Introduced-1996. Retired-1997. Availability-Rare. Sizes: 8, 11, 14 Inch Plates; 9, 11, 14 Inch Bowls; 10, 14 Inch Trays; 6, 8 Inch Roundels. Comments: Someone requested we do the cherub plate as a semi-custom piece. Cherubs were very popular at the time, so we decided to try it in the line.

## MEADOW

By: Diane Johnston.
Introduced-1997. Retired
2004. Availability-
Common. Sizes: 6, 8, 11,
14, 16, 20 Inch Plates; 9,
11, 14, 16 Inch Bowls; 9,
11 Inch Fluted Bowls; 10,
14 Inch Trays; 13 Inch
Square; 10 Inch Heart; 20
Inch Table; 9 Inch Clock;
6, 8 Inch Roundels.
Comments: Meadow was
one of my favorite
patterns; I loved the
hidden butterfly and bee.
Diane liked to include the
letter "E" in a lot of her
designs for her daughter,
Emily. See if you can find
them.

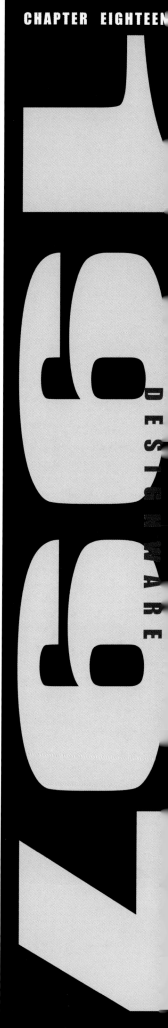

## CHAPTER EIGHTEEN

## DAISIES

By: Beth Ellen Introduced: 1997. Retired-2001. Availability-Common. Sizes: 6, 8, 11, 14, 16, 20 Inch Plates; 9, 11, 14, 16 Inch Bowls; 9, 11 Inch Fluted Bowls; 10, 14 Inch Trays; 13 Inch Square; 10 Inch Heart; 20 Inch Table; 9 Inch Clock; 6, 8 Inch Roundels. Comments: Daisies was a terrific pattern. It did well but had a bubble problem which finally forced us to retire it. We replaced it with a new daisy pattern in 2003.

## ROSES (1997)

By: David Switzer. Introduced-1997. Retired-1998. Availability-Rare. Sizes: 6, 8, 11, 14, 16, 20 Inch Plates; 9, 11, 14, 16 Inch Bowls; 9, 11 Inch Fluted Bowls; 10, 14 Inch Trays; 13 Inch Square; 10 Inch Heart; 9 Inch Clock; 6, 8 Inch Roundels; 20 Inch Table. Comments: We have tried Roses several times, but I think David's attempt was the most successful. The colors he used worked very well together.

## BALLOON (1997)

By: Suzy Arvidson. Introduced-1997. Retired-1997. Availability-Rare. Sizes: 8, 14 Inch Plates; 9 Inch Clock; 6, 8 Inch Roundels. Comments: This plate started out as a semi-custom design which we later decided to try in the line.

## BLUEBONNET

By: Diane Johnston. Introduced-1997. Retired-1997. Availability-Rare. Sizes: 8, 14 Inch Plates; 14 Inch Bowl; 9 Inch Clock; 6, 8 Inch Roundels. Comments: Our Texas accounts had asked many times for a Bluebonnet, so Diane was happy to give them one.

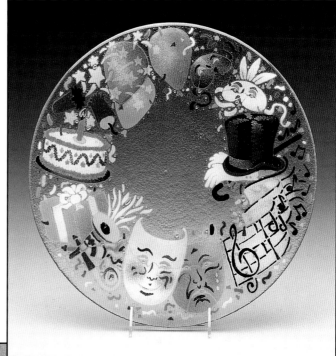

## CELEBRATION

By: David Switzer. Introduced-1997. Retired-2000. Availability-Average. Sizes: 6, 8, 11, 14, 16, 20 Inch Plates; 9, 11, 14, 16 Inch Bowls; 10, 14 Inch Trays; 13 Inch Square; 20 Inch Table. Comments: David had a lot of fun creating this plate. It was purchased and given to the cast and crew of the TV series "Will & Grace" as a special gift. It was also done in "Mardi Gras" colors for a special customer in New Orleans.

## CORAL REEF

By: Donna Orsini DesJadon. Introduced-1997. Retired-2002. Availability-Numerous. Sizes: 6, 8, 11, 14, 16, 20 Inch Plates; 9, 11, 14, 16 Inch Bowls; 10, 14 Inch Trays; 13 Inch Square; 18 Inch Oval; 20 Inch Table; 9 Inch Clock; 6, 8 Inch Roundels. Comments: Donna spent a lot of time researching and deciding which fish to put in this design. Coral Reef was the second tropical fish pattern to be followed in 2003 by Under The Sea. Fish are a natural for fused glass and all the patterns sold very well.

## TRIBAL

By: Ann Mallory. Introduced-1997. Retired-2002. Availability-Average. Sizes: 6, 8, 11, 14, 16, 20 Inch Plates; 9, 11, 14, 16 Inch Bowls; 10, 14 Inch Trays; 13 Inch Square; 20 Inch Table. Comments: Ann was a good friend I had met at a trade show. She is a ceramic artist with her own line of hand-painted dinnerware. We did some contract work for her and later I asked her to design something for us. Tribal was also available in the Judaic line as Seder, Matzo, and Shabbat.

## HOLIDAY COOKIES

By: Suzy Arvidson. Introduced-1997. Retired-2000. Availability-Average. Sizes: 6, 8, 11, 14, 16, 20 Inch Plates; 9, 11, 14, 16 Inch Bowls; 10, 14 Inch Trays; 13 Inch Square; 20 Inch Tables. Comments: The cookies looked so good you could almost taste them. At signing events people would have me sign the names of their children on the different cookies.

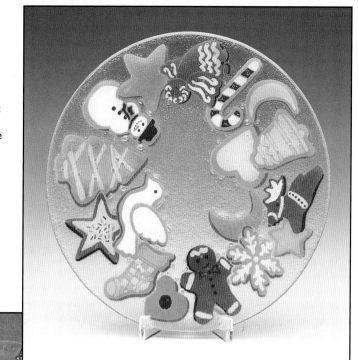

## SKATING POND

By: Suzy Arvidson. Introduced-1997. Retired 1999. Availability-Rare. Sizes: 11 Inch Plate. Comments: Skating Pond was part of a Premier Series using silkscreen techniques to get fine details in the plates. We silk-screened the detail with special black ink I created on the underside of the top piece of glass. Skating Pond was first in a series of seasonal designs using this technique.

## SNOWMAN

By: David Switzer. Introduced-1997. Retired-NA. Availability-Numerous. Sizes: 6, 8, 11, 14, 16, 20 Inch Plates; 9, 11, 14, 16 Inch Bowls; 9, 11 Inch Fluted Bowls; 10, 14, 16 Inch Trays; 18 Inch Oval; 10, 13 Inch Squares; 20 Inch Table; 6, 8 Inch Roundels. Comments: Snowman is David's most successful design. It captures the spirit of winter with this whimsical snowman and his wildlife friends. It's available in almost every size and shape we produce.

## POINSETTIA

By: Diane Johnston. Introduced-1997. Retired-1999. Availability-Average. Sizes: 6, 8, 11, 14, 16, 20 Inch Plates; 9, 11, 14, 16 Inch Bowls; 9, 11 Inch Fluted Bowls; 10, 14 Inch Trays; 13 Inch Square; 6, 8 Inch Roundels; 20 Inch Table. Comments: Poinsettias are such a popular Christmas flower that we have used them in several different designs.

## BOUQUET

By: David Switzer. Intro-
duced-1998. Retired-2000.
Availability-Limited. Sizes: 6,
8, 11, 14, 16, 20 Inch Plates;
9, 11, 14, 16 Inch Bowls; 9,
11 Inch Fluted Bowls; 10, 14
Inch Trays; 13 Inch Square;
10 Inch Heart; 20 Inch Table;
9 Inch Clock; 6 Inch
Roundel. Comments: Pansies
had been such a big hit we
decided to try another floral
pattern with the same
colors; but unfortunately,
Bouquet did not have the
same success.

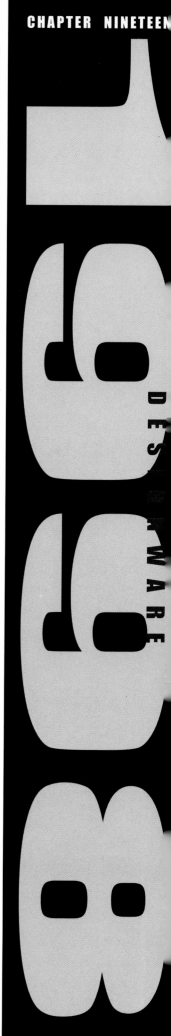

## ROOSTER

By: Diane Johnston. Introduced-1998. Retired-2003. Availability-Common.
Sizes: 6, 8, 11, 14, 16, 20 Inch Plates; 9, 11, 14, 16 Inch Bowls; 9, 11 Inch
Fluted Bowls; 10, 14 Inch Trays; 13 Inch Square; 10 Inch Heart; 16, 20 Inch
Tables; 9 Inch Clock; 6 Inch Roundel. Comments: Rooster had a wonderful
country charm. It included our trademark checkerboard and a pastoral farm
background. If you have ever spent any time up close with a real rooster,
they can be extremely colorful and beautiful. Diane went on to design
another Rooster in 2004 named Chanticleer.

## FESTIVE BIRDS

By: Peggy Karr. Introduced-1998. Retired-2002. Availability-Common. Sizes:
6, 8, 11, 14, 16, 20 Inch Plates; 9, 11, 14, 16 Inch Bowls; 9, 11 Inch Fluted
Bowls; 10, 14 Inch Trays; 13 Inch Square; 16, 20 Inch Tables. Comments: I
have always had a bird feeder outside my bedroom window so I can watch
them in the morning. Festive Birds includes many of my Northeast favorites.

## CHILIES

By: Donna Orsini DesJadon. Introduced-1998. Retired-NA. Availability-Numerous. Sizes: 6, 8, 11, 14, 16, 20 Inch Plates; 9, 11, 14, 16 Inch Bowls; 9, 11 Inch Fluted Bowls; 10, 14, 16 Inch Trays; 18 Inch Oval; 10, 13 Inch Squares; 16, 20 Inch Tables; 9 Inch Clock; 6 Inch Roundel. Comments: Chilies was a bigger hit than we ever thought it would be. We knew it was a popular subject and Donna gave it just the right hot colors in the background.

## SOUTHWEST STILL-LIFE

By: Suzy Arvidson. Introduced-1998. Retired-2000. Availability-Rare. Sizes: 6, 8, 11, 14, 16, 20 Inch Plates; 9, 11, 14, 16 Inch Bowls; 10, 14 Inch Trays; 13 Inch Square; 16, 20 Inch Tables. Comments: Southwest Still-life was a companion piece for our chili pattern. Both worked well together and gave our Southwest customers more than one pattern choice.

## GOLF COURSE

By: Peggy Karr. Introduced-1998. Retired-NA. Availability-Numerous. Sizes: 6, 8, 11, 14, 16, 20 Inch Plates; 9, 11, 14, 16 Inch Bowls; 10, 14 Inch Trays; 13 Inch Square; 16, 20 Inch Tables; 9 Inch Clock; 6 Inch Roundel. Comments: I previously designed two other golf plates and decided I wanted to try once again. The biggest problem was trying to design a Golf Course without having it look like a particular club, which would require special permission. I especially liked the effect of the tree in the foreground of this design.

## YACHTING

By: David Switzer. Introduced-1998. Retired-2000. Availability-Rare. Sizes: 6, 8, 11, 14, 16, 20 Inch Plates; 9, 11, 14, 16 Inch Bowls; 10, 14 Inch Trays; 13 Inch Square; 20 Inch Table; 9 Inch Clock; 6 Inch Roundel. Comments: Yachting was our fourth try at a sailboat theme. We thought that sailing was a good subject and should work well in glass. David made this one more colorful with more boats in a deep blue ocean with a clear sunny sky.

## WOLVES

By: Suzy Arvidson. Introduced-1998. Retired-1999. Availability-Rare. Sizes: 6, 8, 11, 14, 16, 20 Inch Plates; 9, 11, 14, 16 Inch Bowls; 10, 14 Inch Trays; 13 Inch Square; 20 Inch Table; 9 Inch Clock. Comments: There was a wolf preserve with a gift shop not far from our factory . The owner asked if we could do something with wolves, so Suzy created this design with them in mind.

## WITCH

By: Diane Johnston. Introduced-1998. Retired-2002. Availability-Average. Sizes: 11, 14, 16 Inch Plates; 11, 14, 16 Inch Bowls; 13 Inch Square. Comments: The Witch was our second Halloween design. Diane caught her just as she was crossing the moon with her cape and orange hair flowing in the breeze. At signing events I used to love to engrave, "To the Emerald City like lightning" on this plate.

## AUTUMN HOMECOMING

By: David Switzer. Introduced-1998. Retired-1998. Availability-Rare. Sizes: 11 Inch Plate. Comments: Autumn Homecoming was the second in the seasonal Premier Series. It incorporated silk-screened black line detail, giving the design a illustration-like effect.

## NOAH'S ARK

By: David Switzer. Introduced-1998. Retired-1999. Availability-Rare. Sizes: 11 Inch Plate. Comments: Noah's Ark was the last plate in the Premier Series. David's background was in illustration, so he really enjoyed putting all the details into Noah's ark, best utilizing the silkscreen black line technique.

## LOVE HEART

By: Diane Johnston. Introduced-1998. Retired-1998. Availability-Rare. Sizes: 10 Inch Heart. Comments: Sometimes a good idea just doesn't work out as well as you hoped. The concept was great with the word "Love" running around the rim in different languages on a heart-shaped plate but the actual design never worked out very well.

## WREN HEART

By: Diane Johnston. Introduced-1998. Retired-1998. Availability-Rare. Sizes: 10 Inch Heart. Comments: We decided to design things exclusively for the heart shape because not many of our regular patterns fit the shape. We introduced two patterns: The Love Heart and The Wren Heart. These were our only single heart designs.

## PEACE

By: Diane Johnston. Introduced-1998. Retired-1998. Availability-Rare. Sizes: 11 Inch Plate. Comments: Peace was part of the Premier Series. All the detail in both the lion and the lamb came from a black line silkscreen technique we used in the series.

## BRIDE & GROOM

By: Donna Orsini DesJadon. Introduced-1998. Retired-NA. Availability-Numerous. Sizes: 11, 14 Inch Plates. Comments: Our first Wedding plate was done by Mary Kay. We felt it needed to be updated so Donna redesigned it. She added an elegant new dress for the bride with lots of detailed lace and it is still in the line today. It was also available in Judaic called Hebrew Bride and Groom.

## CHAPTER TWENTY

## GARDENING

By: Suzy Arvidson. Intro-
duced-1999. Retired-2000.
Availability-Limited. Sizes: 6,
8, 11, 14, 16, 20 Inch Plates;
9, 11, 14, 16 Inch Bowls; 10,
14 Inch Trays; 13 Inch Square;
20 Inch Table; 9 Inch Clock; 6
Inch Roundel. Comments:
Suzy's parents were avid
gardeners and had given her a
lot of inspiration for this
design.

## TROPICAL FLORAL

By: Donna Orsini DesJadon. Introduced-1999. Retired-NA. Availability-Average. Sizes: 6, 8, 11, 14, 16, 20 Inch Plates; 9, 11, 14, 16 Inch Bowls; 9, 11 Inch Fluted Bowls; 10, 14 Inch Trays; 13 Inch Square; 20 Inch Table; 9 Inch Clock; 6 Inch Roundel. Comments: Tropical Floral was Donna's last design. She spent a lot of time getting it just right. She asked if she could go to Hawaii to gather more research but I told her if anyone was going I was first in line.

## AUTUMN SUNFLOWER

By: Peggy Karr. Introduced-1999. Retired-2003. Availability-Average. Sizes: 6, 8, 11, 14, 16, 20 Inch Plates; 9, 11, 14, 16 Inch Bowls; 9, 11 Inch Fluted Bowls; 10, 14 Inch Trays; 13 Inch Square; 20 Inch Table; 6 Inch Roundel. Comments: We have had several different Autumn patterns but I thought we needed a design that included flowers. After a ton of research I found that sunflowers went well with autumn themes, so I added the colored leaves around the border. In 2001 we took out the Sunflowers and added a Turkey to the center of the plate for Thanksgiving.

## CIRCLE OF HOPE

By: David Switzer. Introduced-1999. Retired-1999. Availability-Average. Sizes: 11, 14 Inch Plates. Comments: We originally designed this plate for The Children's Hospital of Omaha's fiftieth anniversary. The hospital liked the design so much they used it on all their stationary for the anniversary celebration. We made the plates available to all our customers after the event and donated a portion of the profits back to the hospital.

## CIRCUS

By: Diane Johnston. Introduced-1999. Retired-1999. Availability-Rare. Sizes: 11, 14 Inch Plates; 14, 16 Inch Trays; . Comments: Diane captured the spirit of a circus with these Harlequin acrobats and traditional elephants decked out in their finest costumes.

## WATERFOWL

By: David Switzer. Introduced-1999. Retired-2000. Availability-Rare. Sizes: 11, 14 Inch Plates; 14, 16 Inch Trays; 10, 13 Inch Squares. Comments: David's waterfowl almost looked real. He created a wonderful effect with their reflections in the water, which made them come to life.

## SERENGETI

By. Suzy Arvidson. Introduced-1999. Retired-2002. Availability-Rare. Sizes: 11, 14 Inch Plates; 14, 16 Inch Trays; 10, 13 Inch Squares. Comments: The Serengeti series was Suzy's last design. There were originally three different scenes: Cheetah, Giraffe, and Zebra. I later added the Elephant. The different African inspired patterned borders gave them a lot of character.

## BELL ROCK

By: Staff. Introduced-1999. Retired-1999. Availability-Rare. Sizes: 11, 14 Inch Plates. Comments: This was a collaborative effort of our art department. Everyone contributed their specialties to create this design. Bell Rock is located outside Sedona, Arizona.

## HORSES

By: Peggy Karr. Introduced-1999. Retired-1999. Availability-Rare. Sizes: 11, 14 Inch Plates. Comments: Because of my love of horses, all of my friends kept asking for a horse plate. It was hard coming up with something that looked good because horses are not very colorful. I would like to give it another try sometime soon.

## SHAMROCKS

By: Diane Johnston. Introduced-1999. Retired-
NA. Availability-Common. Sizes: 11, 14 Inch
Plates; 9, 14 Inch Bowls; 14, 16 Inch Trays.
Comments: Shamrocks is a simple design that
fits the bill for St. Patrick's Day and a general
Irish plate. We have added sizes to meet the
demand of Irish fans. We never expected it to
do as well as it has.

## STARS & STRIPES

By: Diane Johnston. Introduced-1999. Retired-
2002. Availability-Average. Sizes: 11, 14 Inch
Plates; 9, 14 Inch Bowls; 14, 16 Inch Trays.
Comments: Stars & Stripes was the first pattern
that Diane designed directly on the computer.
Although we had been computerized for quite
a while, the designers still drew the designs by
hand and then Billy entered the drawings into
the computer.

## SLEIGH (1999)

By: David Switzer. Introduced-1999. Retired-2000. Availability-Limited.
Sizes: 6, 8, 11, 14, 16, 20 Inch Plates; 9, 11, 14, 16 Inch Bowls; 10, 14 Inch
Trays; 13 Inch Square; 20 Inch Table; 6 Inch Roundel. Comments: Sleigh was
our second Santa and reindeer design. The first one in 1993 had Santa flying
over a sleepy little village and this one was a closer view of Santa taking off
from the roof. You can even see his footprints in the snow.

## 12 DAYS

By: David Switzer. Introduced-1999. Retired-1999. Availability-Rare. Sizes: 11, 14 Inch Plates; 9 Inch Clock. Comments: I still can't believe David was able to get all those elements into one plate and it also looked fabulous in a clock. Later in 2000 we did a plate based only on the partridge and pear tree.

## MILLENIUM-SPACE

By: Suzy Arvidson. Introduced-1999. Retired-1999. Availability-Rare. Sizes: 11, 14 Inch Plates . Comments: We couldn't let the millennium pass without commemorating it with a plate. Millennium space depicted our fiery solar system.

## MILLENNIUM-TIME

By: Diane Johnston. Introduced-1999. Retired-1999. Availability-Rare. Sizes: 11, 14 Inch Plates. Comments: There were two different Millennium plates. This one was Millennium Time, which captured the essence of time passing.

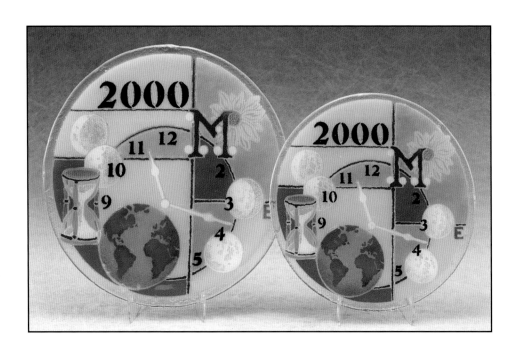

## CHAPTER TWENTY-ONE

## HYDRANGEA (2000 COLLECTIBLE)

By: Peggy Karr. Introduced-2000. Retired-2000. Availability-Average. Sizes: 11 Inch Plate. Comments: Hydrangea was the first in our Limited Edition Collectible Series. Each of these plates is signed, dated, and numbered by me personally and comes with a certificate of authenticity. At first we weren't sure if a collectible series would be a success, but it turned out to be the best selling 11" plate for that year. This plate was limited to production in the year 2000 only.

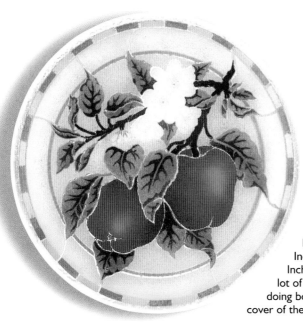

## APPLES

By: Peggy Karr. Introduced-2000. Retired-2002. Availability-Average. Sizes: 6, 8, 11, 14, 16, 20 Inch Plates; 9, 11, 14 Inch Bowls; 9, 11 Inch Fluted Bowls; 10, 14, 16 Inch Trays; 10, 13 Inch Squares; 16, 20 Inch Tables. Comments: I had a lot of fun designing Apples as I have always enjoyed doing botanicals. It looked so good we used it on the cover of the wholesale catalog that year.

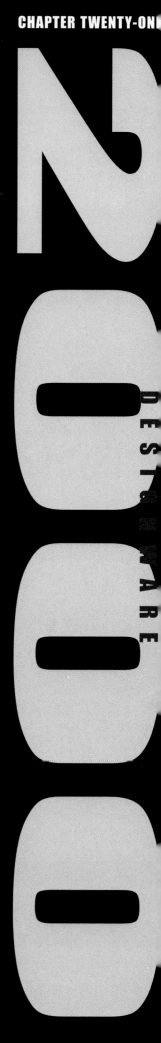

## GOURMET GARDEN

By: Diane Johnston. Introduced-2000. Retired-NA. Availability-
Common. Sizes: 11, 14 Inch Plates; 9, 11, 14 Inch Bowls; 10 Inch Tray;
18 Inch Oval; 13 Inch Square. Comments: Gourmet Garden is Diane's
second vegetable design. One of Diane's favorite vegetables is
eggplant and at first she had it covering almost half the plate. We had
to talk her into making it a little smaller.

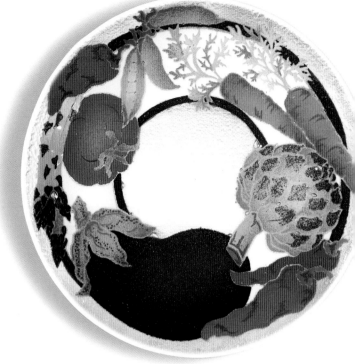

## WELCOME PINEAPPLE

By: Yolanda V. Fundora. Introduced-2000. Retired-2001. Availability-
Rare. Sizes: 8, 11, 14 Inch Plates; 10, 13 Inch Squares. Comments:
Dating back to colonial America, the Pineapple has long remained a
symbol of hospitality and friendship. We did a special version of
Pineapple for Hawaii that said Aloha instead of Welcome. We used
the same pineapple in a later design with a Bombay theme in 2004.

## TULIPS

By: David Switzer. Introduced-2000. Retired-NA. Availability-Average. Sizes: 6, 8, 11, 14 Inch Plates; 9, 11, 14 Inch Bowls; 9, 11 Inch Fluted Bowls; 10, 13 Inch Squares. Comments: We had originally designed Tulips as a plate for a QVC special hosted by Phyllis George on American Crafts. We liked the plate so much we changed it around a little and added it to our line.

## SINGING BIRD

By: Yolanda V. Fundora. Introduced-2000. Retired-2000. Availability-Rare. Sizes: 8, 11, 14 Inch Plates. Comments: Singing Bird was one of Yolanda's first designs. It was reminiscent of Heartland, created in 1994 by Salli-Ann.

## CHERRIES

By: Yolanda V. Fundora. Introduced-2000. Retired-2001. Availability-Rare. Sizes: 8, 11, 14 Inch Plates; 9, 11, 14 Inch Bowls; 9, 11 Inch Fluted Bowls. Comments: Yolanda had just joined the company as Art Director and was able to adapt quickly to overcome the challenges involved in designing for fused glass. Cherries was one of her first designs.

## BLUE FRUIT

By: David Switzer. Introduced-2000. Retired-2000. Availability-Rare. Sizes: 8, 11, 14 Inch Plates; 9, 11, 14 Inch Bowls. Comments: Blue Fruit was a very unusual design. We all loved it, but it was too out of character for our customers and very few pieces were produced. If you own one, you should hold on to it.

## PERSIAN BLUES

By: Yolanda V. Fundora. Introduced-2000. Retired-NA. Availability-Rare. Sizes: 8, 11, 14, 16 Inch Plates; 9, 11, 14 Inch Bowls; 18 Inch Oval. Comments: Persian Blues is one of Yolanda's favorites. While its appeal to our customers is limited, the people who love it ... REALLY love it. Persian Blue was also available in the Judaic line as a Seder, Matzo, and Shabbat.

## SEASHELLS (2000)

By: Diane Johnston. Introduced-2000. Retired-NA. Availability-Average. Sizes: 8, 11, 14, 16, 20 Inch Plates; 9, 11, 14 Inch Bowls; 9, 11 Inch Fluted Bowls; 10, 14, 16 Inch Trays; 18 Inch Oval; 10, 13 Inch Squares; 16, 20 Inch Tables. Comments: Seashells captures the soft pastel colors of shells found along the beach. Diane added the sea fans and blue coral as the perfect background for the shells.

## KOKOPELLI

By: Peggy Karr. Introduce-2000. Retired-2002. Availability-Limited. Sizes: 11, 14 Inch Plates; 10, 14 Inch Trays; 10, 13 Inch Squares. Comments: Everyone thought we needed a new Southwest design. It was a lot of fun researching the Indian symbols and myths for the plate. The name "Kokopelli" comes from the Hopi Indians and is thought to be a fertility symbol. The character dates back to the Anasazi, but no one is clear about its actual origins or what he originally represented.

## MOOSE

By: David Switzer. Introduced-2000. Retired-2000. Availability-Rare. Sizes: 11, 14 Inch Plates; 14, 16 Inch Trays. Comments: Customers in the Northwest were asking for a Moose plate so David created this moose in his natural environment. In 2002, I designed another moose, which had more of a "lodge" look and was appropriately called Lodge Moose.

## PINECONE

By: Bill Brisley. Introduced-2000. Retired-2002. Availability-Rare. Sizes: 11, 14 Inch Plates; 10, 13 Inch Squares. Comments: Pinecone was Billy's first design and he spent a lot of time getting it just right. It captured the feeling of a Northwest pine forest perfectly.

## POPPIES

By: Diane Johnston. Introduced-2000. Retired-2002. Availability-Limited. Sizes: 8, 11, 14, 16 Inch Plates; 9, 11, 14 Inch Bowls; 10, 13 Inch Squares; 16 Inch Table. Comments: Poppies had an Oriental feel. It originally had an unusual solid background, which we took out because we felt the clear glass looked better.

## ORNAMENTS

By: Yolanda V. Fundora. Introduced-2000. Retired-2002. Availability-Limited. Sizes: 11, 14 Inch Plates; 10 Inch Tray; 18 Inch Oval. Comments: Ornaments was our second design using these colorful Christmas decorations as the subject. Yolanda's choice of bright, primary colors makes this design even more festive.

## PARTRIDGE IN A PEAR TREE

By: Diane Johnston. Introduced-2000. Retired-2002. Availability-Rare. Sizes: 11, 14 Inch Plates; 10, 13 Inch Squares. Comments: Partridge In A Pear Tree was going to be the first in a series. We thought about adding more from The Twelve Days of Christmas but felt the Partridge was the only one that everyone would easily recognize. Its rich red background and the details given to the Partridge made it a very elegant plate.

## HOLLY

By: Yolanda V. Fundora. Introduced-2000. Retired-2001. Availability-Rare. Sizes: 6, 8, 11, 14, 16 Inch Plates; 9, 11, 14 Inch Bowls; 9, 11 Inch Fluted Bowls; 10, 14, 16 Inch Trays; 10, 13 Inch Squares. Comments: Yolanda designed with a lot of clear glass in her first designs. That can sometimes make it very difficult to control the bubbles and Holly was no exception.

## COYOTE CHRISTMAS

By: David Switzer. Introduced-2000. Retired-2002. Availability-Rare. Sizes: 8, 11, 14 Inch Plates. Comments: David's style was designing with lots of detail, which he always enjoys. He managed to fit an entire desert decked out for Christmas on this plate.

## CONVERSATION HEARTS

By: Yolanda V. Fundora. Introduced-2000. Retired-2002. Availability-Average. Sizes: 8, 11, 14 Inch Plates; 9 Inch Bowl; 10 Inch Heart. Comments: Yolanda brought a fresh new approach to our designs. Conversation Hearts were a lot of fun and brought back memories of those little "message" candies for Valentine's Day.

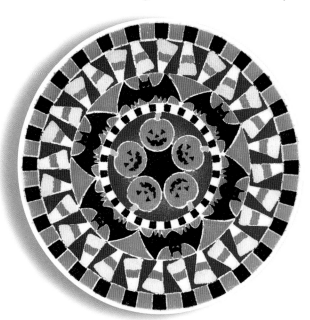

## TRICK OR TREAT

By: Yolanda V. Fundora. Introduced-2000. Retired-2002. Availability-Rare. Sizes: 8, 11, 14 Inch Plates; 9, 11, 14 Inch Bowls; 10, 13 Inch Squares. Comments: Trick or Treat was our third Halloween design. It was a graphic treatment of Halloween featuring fun candy corn, pumpkins and little bats, all of which create the fun illusion of a kaleidoscope.

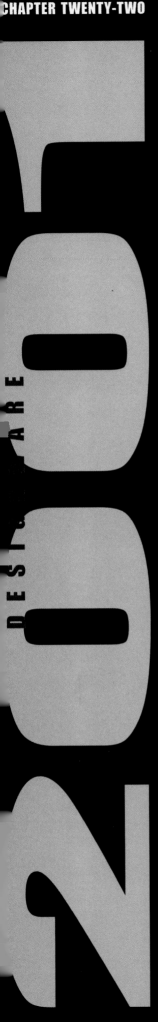

## CHAPTER TWENTY-TWO

### CALLA LILY (2001 COLLECTIBLE)

By: Peggy Karr. Introduced-2001. Retired-2001. Availability-Common. Sizes: 11 Inch Plate. Comments: Calla Lily was the second in the Limited Edition Collectible Series. It was personally signed, dated, and numbered by me and came with a certificate of authenticity. This plate was limited to production in the year 2001.

### GEISHA

By: Yolanda V. Fundora. Introduced-2001. Retired-2002. Availability-Rare. Sizes: 11, 14 Inch Plates; 10, 14 Inch Trays; 10, 13 Inch Squares. Comments: The "Geisha" is Japanese for "Art Person". They are trained for many years in singing, dancing, and entertaining. I created a new color called ocean that can be seen in the sky.

### DAFFODILS

By: Diane Johnston. Introduced-2001. Retired-2004. Availability-Average. Sizes: 8, 11, 14 Inch Plates; 9, 11, 14 Inch Bowls; 9, 11 Inch Fluted Bowls; 10, 14 Inch Trays; 10, 13 Inch Squares; 10 Inch Heart; 20 Inch Table. Comments: The sunny yellow Daffodils, white Narcissus, and little Grape Hyacinths bring a smile to your face. Diane captured the season of Spring with these lovely flowers.

## MORNING GLORIES

By: Yolanda V. Fundora. Introduced-2001. Retired-NA. Availability-Average. Sizes: 6, 8, 11, 14 Inch Plates; 9, 11, 14 Inch Bowls; 9, 11 Inch Fluted Bowls; 18 Inch Oval; 10 Inch Square; 10 Inch Heart; 20 Inch Table. Comments: Morning Glories was an all around hit for Yolanda, it sold well, had no technical problems, was easy to make, and is still in the line today. Morning Glories were also available in the Judaic line as a Seder, Matzo, and Shabbat.

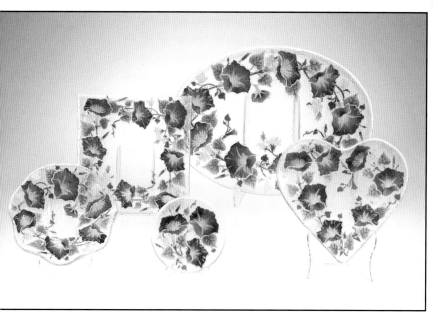

## GERANIUMS

By: Diane Johnston. Introduced-2001. Retired-NA. Availability-Common. Sizes: 8, 11, 14 Inch Plates; 9, 11, 14 Inch Bowls; 10, 13 Inch Squares. Comments: Diane spends a lot of her free time caring for her garden. Geraniums are among her favorite flowers, so they were the perfect fit for a design. The intricate leaves make the design very realistic.

## SEAFOOD

By: Diane Johnston. Introduced-2001. Retired-NA. Availability-Limited. Sizes: 8, 11, 14, 16, 20 Inch Plates; 9, 11, 14 Inch Bowls; 10, 14 Inch Trays; 18 Inch Oval; 10, 13 Inch Squares. Comments: You can almost taste these seafood favorites dipped in melted butter. The shell pattern around the outside rim of the plate frames the bright red lobster and crabs in the center.

## ORCHARD

By: Peggy Karr. Introduced-2001. Retired-2004. Availability-Average. Sizes: 8, 11, 14 Inch Plates; 9, 11, 14 Inch Bowls; 10, 14 Inch Trays; 18 Inch Oval; 10, 13 Inch Squares. Comments: Fruit has been a very strong category for us, starting with the Checkerboard Fruit design in 1988. It was a real challenge to fill in all the empty space around the fruit with leaves so the plate wouldn't bubble. I designed Orchard as a replacement for Harvest Fruit.

## SERENGETI-ELEPHANT

By: Peggy Karr. Introduced-2001. Retired-2002. Availability-Rare. Sizes: 11, 14 Inch Plates. Comments: I designed the Elephant to go with the rest of the Serengeti pieces designed by Suzy. I created a special color, taupe, just for the elephant so she and her baby would look realistic.

## ANIMAL FROLICS

By: Yolanda V. Fundora. Introduced-2001. Retired-2004. Availability-Limited. Sizes: 11, 14 Inch Plates; 10, 14 Inch Trays; 10, 13 Inch Squares; 10 Inch Heart. Comments: Animal Frolics was a whimsical departure from our regular designs. It was more playful and simple in its graphic treatment of the animals. There were flying bunnies on our square shapes, stacked farm animals on rectangles, and cute kitties on the round shapes.

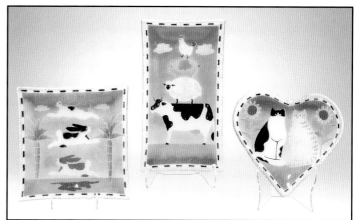

## EASTER EGGS

By: Bill Brisley. Introduced-2001. Retired-2002. Availability-Rare. Sizes: 8, 11, 14 Inch Plates; 9, 11, 14 Inch Bowls; 10, 13 Inch Squares. Comments: Billy spent a lot of time working on the Easter Eggs plate. It may look like a simple design, but there were many different colors with lots of shading that created a challenge when laying out the stencils and for our decorators.

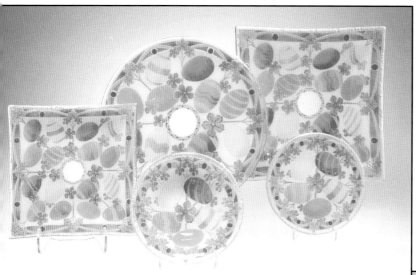

## FLAMINGOS

By: Yolanda V. Fundora. Introduced-2001. Retired-2002. Availability-Rare. Sizes: 8, 11, 14 Inch Plates; 9, 11, 14 Inch Bowls; 20 Inch Table. Comments: Yolanda's Flamingos is our second Flamingo design. I designed the first one back in 1987; it was part of the checkerboard series.

## TOPIARY

By: Bill Brisley. Introduced-2001. Retired-2001.
Availability-Rare. Sizes: 11, 14 Inch Plates; 10, 14
Inch Trays; . Comments: Topiary is the art of
clipping and training plants and trees to grow into
desired shapes. The word comes from the Latin
word Topiarus, which means landscape gardener
and dates back more than 2, 000 years. Billy used
the new ocean blue in his sky.

## BALLOONS (2001)

By: Yolanda V. Fundora. Introduced-2001.
Retired-2002. Availability-Rare. Sizes: 8, 11,
14 Inch Plates; 9, 11, 14 Inch Bowls; 10 Inch
Square. Comments: Balloons was a
combination of our old pattern Stars and
new, colorful balloons. Stars had been a
popular pattern for such a long time we
decided to add the balloons for a more
festive look.

## TURKEY

By: Yolanda V. Fundora. Introduced-2001. Retired-NA.
Availability-Average. Sizes: 14, 16, 20 Inch Plates; 18
Inch Oval. Comments: Yolanda designed Turkey using
the red and orange leaf border from Autumn
Sunflower. That would allow people to mix and match
the smaller Autumn Sunflower pieces with the Turkey
serving platters.

## FATHER CHRISTMAS

By: David Switzer. Introduced-2001. Retired-2002. Availability-Limited. Sizes: 8, 11, 14, 16, 20 Inch Plates; 9, 11, 14 Inch Bowls; 20 Inch Table. Comments: David really enjoys designing plates for Christmas, which can be seen in all the rich details he added throughout this design.

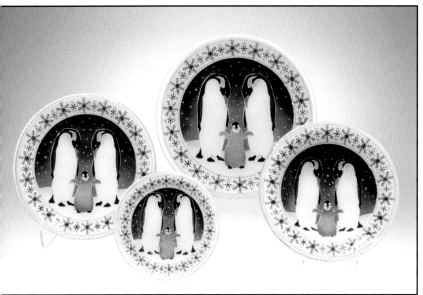

## PENGUINS

By: Yolanda V. Fundora. Introduced-2001. Retired-2002. Availability-Rare. Sizes: 8, 11, 14 Inch Plates; 9, 11, 14 Inch Bowls. Comments: We used these adorable Emperor Penguins to pose for "Baby's First Christmas" in this plate. Emperor Penguins are devoted parents and care for their single chick for many months during the harsh conditions of the South Pole.

## SANTA TREE

By: Yolanda V. Fundora. Introduced-2001. Retired-NA. Availability-Numerous. Sizes: 14 Inch Tree. Comments: The tree shape was introduced in 2001 along with this new design. This whimsical Santa looked perfect on the new shape.

## CHRISTMAS TREE

By: Peggy Karr. Introduced-2001. Retired-2002. Availability-Limited. Sizes: 14 Inch Tree. Comments: I was spending more time creating new shapes for our glass and I thought a Christmas Tree would make a great new addition for our Holiday designs. Naturally, the first one had to have ornaments on it.

## CHAPTER TWENTY-THREE

**2002 DESIGNWARE**

### ROSE (2002 COLLECTIBLE)

By: Peggy Karr. Introduced-2002. Retired-2002. Availability-Average. Sizes: 11 Inch Plate. Comments: The Rose is the third in the Limited Edition Collectible Series. I chose the yellow rose of friendship rather than the red rose because I like the idea of promoting friendship throughout the world. It was personally signed, dated, and numbered by me and came with a certificate of authenticity. This plate was limited to production in the year 2002.

### LEMON

By: Peggy Karr. Introduced-2002. Retired-NA. Availability-Average. Sizes: 8, 11, 14, 20 Inch Plates; 9, 11, 14 Inch Bowls; 10, 14 Inch Trays; 10, 13 Inch Squares; 20 Inch Table. Comments: Lemons just popped into my head one day and I designed it just as quickly. Some designs seem to come naturally while others I struggle with for a long time. I enjoy doing botanicals and like the way the border of sliced and whole lemons compliments the center.

## WINE

By: Peggy Karr. Introduced-2002. Retired-NA. Availability-Numerous. Sizes: 8, 11, 14 Inch Plates; 9, 11, 14 Inch Bowls; 10, 14 Inch Trays; 18 Inch Oval; 10, 13 Inch Squares; 16 Inch Table. Comments: We were visiting one of our sales representatives in Minneapolis and it was suggested I try a design using wine as the subject. I came home and dashed off this design just in time to get into the catalog. It was an immediate success, becoming our number one pattern that year.

## STRAWBERRIES

By: Yolanda V. Fundora. Introduced-2002. Retired-NA. Availability-Limited. Sizes: 8, 11, 14 Inch Plates; 9, 11, 14 Inch Bowls; 10 Inch Tray; 10 Inch Square. Comments: We often talked about designing a berry plate but never created one we liked until Yolanda designed Strawberries. Its first name was Strawberries and Cream, but we shortened it to just Strawberries when we put it in the catalog.

## NASTURTIUMS

By: Diane Johnston. Introduced-2002. Retired-2004. Availability-Rare. Sizes: 8, 11, 14 Inch Plates; 9, 11, 14 Inch Bowls; 10, 14 Inch Trays; 18 Inch Oval. Comments: Nasturtiums are one of only a few flowers that are edible. You can grow them in your backyard and add them to your salads or deserts for some dramatic color. Diane was able to capture these wonderful delicacies in glass.

## CHERRY BLOSSOMS

By: Yolanda V. Fundora. Introduced-2002. Retired-2004. Availability-Limited. Sizes: 6, 8, 11, 14 Inch Plates; 9, 11, 14 Inch Bowls; 9, 11 Inch Fluted Bowls; 10, 14 Inch Trays; 10 Inch Square; 10 Inch Heart. Comments: Yolanda wanted to carry the theme from the Geisha plate into the Cherry Blossom design, so she used the same blue background in both plates as well as the pink and white cherry blossoms.

## BUNNIES

By: Diane Johnston. Introduced-2002. Retired-NA. Availability-Average. Sizes: 6, 8, 11, 14 Inch Plates; 9, 11 Inch Bowls; 10, 14 Inch Trays; 10, 13 Inch Squares; 10 Inch Heart. Comments: We retired Suzie's Rabbits in 2001 and felt it was time to come out with a new bunny pattern. Diane also chose the traditional white rabbit for her plates.

## SWANS (2002)

By: David Switzer. Introduced-2002. Retired-2002. Availability-Rare. Sizes: 8, 11, 14 Inch Plates. Comments: One of our employees was getting married and asked David to design an ornament she could give to her guests as a favor. We decided to try Swans again, the first swan was designed by Mary Kay in 1991.

## SCHOONER

By: David Switzer. Introduced-2002. Retired-2002. Availability-Rare. Sizes: 11, 14, 16 Inch Plates; 18 Inch Oval. Comments: Schooner was our fifth and final attempt at a sailing plate. It was a beautiful plate and Dave created such an incredible sky, but unfortunately this one has gone the way of the others.

## FISH FROLICS

By: Yolanda V. Fundora. Introduced-2002. Retired-2004. Availability-Limited. Sizes: 11, 14, 20 Inch Plates; 9, 11, 14 Inch Bowls; 18 Inch Oval; 20 Inch Table; 11 Inch Fish. Comments: Yolanda designed Fish Frolics with the same style she used with Animal Frolics. I created another new mold in the shape of a fish so she put the same three colorful fish from the design onto the new shape. They were extremely cute with their big red lips.

add food & drink

pool goes here

call your friends

The fun starts with Peggy Karr Glass

PEGGY KARR GLASS

## SUN & MOON (2002)

By: Yolanda V. Fundora. Introduced-2002. Retired-2004. Availability-Limited. Sizes: 8, 11, 14 Inch Plates; 20 Inch Table. Comments: This is our second Sun & Moon pattern. Yolanda's version was more graphic, but still captured the charming faces of the Sun and Moon as in Diane's version from 1993.

## CARDS

By: Diane Johnston. Introduced-2002. Retired-NA. Availability-Average. Sizes: 6, 8, 11, 14 Inch Plates; 9, 11, 14 Inch Bowls; 10, 14 Inch Trays. Comments: Diane came up with this great idea to do something with playing cards. It was more popular than we thought it would be. The biggest problem was the care you had to take enameling all those little details in the jack, queen, and king.

## LODGE-MOOSE

By: Peggy Karr. Introduced-2002. Retired-NA. Availability-Rare. Sizes: 8, 11, 14 Inch Plates; 9, 11, 14 Inch Bowls; 10, 14 Inch Trays; 20 Inch Table. Comments: I designed Lodge-Moose in response to all the requests we kept getting from our customers in the Northwest. I particularly like the pine branch border.

## LODGE-TROUT

By: David Switzer. Introduced-2002. Retired-NA. Availability-Rare. Sizes: 11, 14 Inch Plates; 10, 14 Inch Rectangle; 18 Inch Oval; 20 Inch Table. Comments: David finally got to do his trout plate in style. He had the fish perfected from an earlier pattern he created. This time he designed a border of "Fishing Flies" which sets off the colorful trout perfectly.

## PANDA

By: Yolanda V. Fundora. Introduced-2002. Retired-2002. Availability-Rare. Sizes: 8, 11, 14 Inch Plates. Comments: Yolanda designed this plate with the San Diego Zoo in mind. They had just had the birth of Hua Mei, the only Panda cub born in the USA. Later that year, while on vacation, I was able to see Hua Mei.

## POINSETTIA (2002)

By: Yolanda V. Fundora. Introduced-2002. Retired-2004. Availability-Rare. Sizes: 8, 11, 14 Inch Plates; 9, 11, 14 Inch Bowls; 10, 14 Inch Trays; 18 Inch Oval. Comments: Poinsettia was designed in a fifties style. It reminds me of a tablecloth my grandmother used during the holiday season.

## SNOWGUY TREE

By: Yolanda V. Fundora. Introduced-2002. Retired-NA. Availability-Common. Sizes: 14 Inch Tree. Comments: The name "Snowguy" came from the fact that we already had a snowman design and didn't want to cause any confusion. Yolanda created this second tree plate in the same style as the first Santa Tree from 2001.

## SNOWFLAKES

By: Dave Switzer. Introduced-2002. Retired-NA. Availability-Common. Sizes: 6, 8, 11, 14, 20 Inch Plates; 9, 11, 14 Inch Bowls; 9, 11 Inch Fluted Bowls; 10, 14 Inch Trays; 18 Inch Oval; 10, 13 Inch Squares; 20 Inch Table. Comments: This elaborate all over design shows the detailed nature and the uniqueness of each snowflake.

## BULBS TREE

By: Bill Brisley. Introduced-2002. Retired-NA. Availability-Average. Sizes: 14 Inch Tree. Comments: I can still remember burning my fingers after my father warned me not to touch the Christmas bulbs. The newer twinkle lights of today may be safer, but I think they lack the charm of those old bulbs. Billy used them in a graphic treatment for our Christmas tree shape. In 2003, he expanded the design into a regular line.

## HAUNTED HOUSE

By: Peggy Karr. Introduced-2002. Retired-NA. Availability-Average. Sizes: 12 Inch House. Comments: Basically I created the new house shape so I could design a haunted house. It was fun combining all the elements, trying to make the house look scary.

## BOO!

By: Yolanda V. Fundora. Introduced-2002. Retired-2004. Availability-Limited. Sizes: 6, 8, 11, 14 Inch Plates; 9, 11, 14 Inch Bowls; 10, 14 Inch Trays; 10, 13 Inch Squares. Comments: Yolanda had so much fun designing Trick or Treat that she wanted to do another Halloween pattern in 2002.

## GINGERBREAD HOUSE

By: David Switzer. Introduced-2002. Retired-NA. Availability-Common. Sizes: 12 Inch House. Comments: David liked the new house shape and immediately saw it as a gingerbread house. He had lots of fun designing his roof with colorful mint candies.

## HEARTS & ROSES

By: Yolanda V. Fundora. Introduced-2002. Retired-2004. Availability-Rare. Sizes: 8, 11, 14 Inch Plates; 9 Inch Bowl; 10 Inch Heart. Comments: Hearts & Roses was originally designed to replace the Heart pattern we retired in 2001. I thought the little hearts and roses were much prettier than the original Heart pattern, but everyone disagreed, so in 2003 we designed another heart pattern that closely resembled the first.

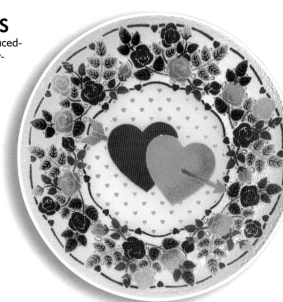

## CHAPTER TWENTY-FOUR

## PETUNIA (2003 COLLECTIBLE)

By: Peggy Karr. Introduced-2003. Retired-2003.
Availability-Average. Sizes: 11 Inch Plate.
Comments: Petunia is the fourth plate in the
Limited Edition Collectable Series. I
personally sign, date, and number each
piece and they each come with a
certificate of authenticity. This plate
was limited to production in the year
2003 only.

## RAINBOW IRIS

By: Yolanda V. Fundora. Introduced-
2003. Retired-NA. Availability-
Limited. Sizes: 8, 11, 14 Inch Plates;
10, 14 Inch Trays; 10 Inch Square.
Comments: My Iris plate had been
around since 1989, so Yolanda
decided to try a new approach to the
flower that captures more of the
beautiful colors and shapes of the Iris.

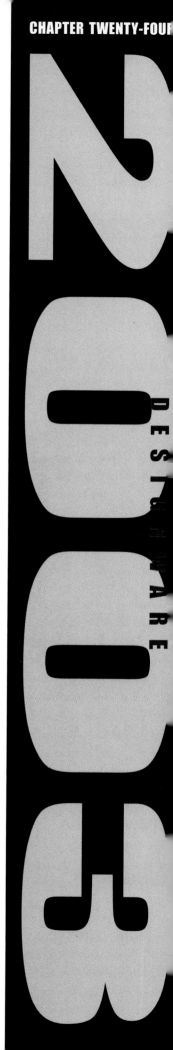

## RED ROSES

By: Yolanda V. Fundora. Introduced-2003. Retired-NA. Availability-Rare. Sizes: 6, 8, 11, 14 Inch Plates; 9, 11 Inch Fluted Bowls; 10, 14 Inch Trays; 10 Inch Square; 10 Inch Heart. Comments: Red Roses is our third rose plate. We keep trying to design different rose patterns for those real rose lovers or as something more romantic for Valentine's Day.

## DAISIES (2003)

By: David Switzer. Introduced-2003. Retired-NA. Availability-Limited. Sizes: 6, 8, 11, 14, 20 Inch Plates; 9, 11, 14 Inch Bowls; 10, 14 Inch Trays; 18 Inch Oval; 10 Inch Heart; 20 Inch Table. Comments: This plate is our second Daisy pattern. Beth had designed the first one in 1997 and we had to retire it early due to technical bubble problems we weren't able to fix. In this rendition David completely covered the plate with flowers in order to avoid any of the bubble problems.

## ROSE OF SHARON

By: Diane Johnston. Introduced-2003. Retired-2003. Availability-Rare. Sizes: 8, 11, 14 Inch Plates; 10 Inch Tray; 18 Inch Oval; 10 Inch Square. Comments: Rose of Sharon was a beautiful plate. When Diane first designed it there was a black background that looked very dramatic. We were all drawn to it but we were concerned the black was too strong so we changed it to blue. The old saying "too many cooks spoil the pot" is true. I think if we had gone with our first instinct, it might have been a better seller.

# TUSCANY

By: Diane Johnston. Introduced-2003. Retired-NA. Availability-Common. Sizes: 6, 8, 11, 14, 20 Inch Plates; 9, 11, 14 Inch Bowls; 10, 14 Inch Trays; 18 Inch Oval; 10 Inch Square; 20 Inch Table. Comments: Tuscany has been a huge success. Diane captured the colors and feel of a Tuscan olive orchard with the traditional Sunflowers usually found in village countryside's. The theme is so popular we plan to add companion pieces to this line in 2005.

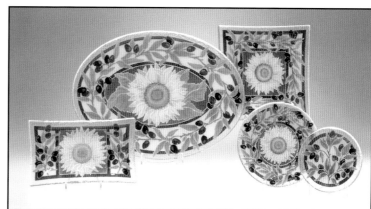

# UNDER THE SEA

By: Yolanda V. Fundora. Introduced-2003. Retired-NA. Availability-Average. Sizes: 8, 11, 14, 20 Inch Plates; 9, 11, 14 Inch Bowls; 10, 14 Inch Trays; 18 Inch Oval; 20 Inch Tables; 11 Inch Fish. Comments: Under the Sea is our third tropical fish plate. Yolanda had just come back from snorkeling while on vacation at a tropical island and was inspired to design a new plate. She had taken pictures underwater and used them to create her design.

## WINDOW CAT

By: Peggy Karr. Introduced-2003. Retired-NA. Availability-Limited. Sizes: 8, 11, 14 Inch Plates; 10, 14 Inch Trays; 10 Inch Square. Comments: Everyone missed Garden Cat when it was retired, so I wanted to do another cat plate. Sometimes it is very easy for me to come up with ideas and other times it seems impossible. I must have gone through at least five versions before I settled on this one. I think Billy was going to kill me if I had him cut one more set of cat stencils.

## TEES

By: Yolanda V. Fundora. Introduced-2003. Retired-NA. Availability-Limited. Sizes: 8, 11, 14 Inch Plates; 9 Inch Bowls; 10 Inch Tray; 20 Inch Table. Comments: I had designed Golf Course in 1998 and we all felt we needed a more colorful golf design, so Yolanda created Tees with all those bright multicolored tees in the border around a golf scene.

# COOKIES

By: Yolanda V. Fundora. Introduced-2003. Retired-NA. Availability-Limited. Sizes: 6, 8, 11, 14 Inch Plates; 9, 11, 14 Inch Bowls; 10 Inch Tray; 10 Inch Square. Comments: Cookies is our second Christmas cookie pattern. Yolanda's design features different cookies covering the plate. In 1997, Suzy used cookies as a border for her design.

# CARDINALS

By: David Switzer. Introduced-2003. Retired-NA. Availability-Limited. Sizes: 8, 11, 14 Inch Plates; 10 Inch Tray; 10 Inch Square. Comments: Not every plate we design makes it into the catalog. Although Dave had designed several different plates with a bird house as part of the subject, none of them had made it into the line. The Cardinals, however, were so cute we had to put them into the catalog

## ROOFTOP SANTA

By: Y. Fundora & B. Brisley. Introduced-2003. Retired-NA. Availability-Limited. Sizes: 8, 11, 14, 20 Inch Plates; 10, 14 Inch Trays; 18 Inch Oval; 20 Inch Table. Comments: Rooftop Santa was a collaborative effort of both Yolanda and Billy. Billy had designed a Winter Scene with this Victorian border that we decided not to produce. Yolanda loved the border and used it to frame her Rooftop Santa.

## BULBS

By: Billy Brisley. Introduced-2003. Retired-NA. Availability-Limited. Sizes: 8, 11, 14 Inch Plates; 9, 11, 14 Inch Bowls; 10, 14 Inch Trays; 18 Inch Oval. Comments: Billy had designed the Bulbs to go on our new tree shape last year and we decided to expand it into a complete line.

## ORNAMENTS TREE

By: David Switzer. Introduced-2003. Retired-NA. Availability-Average. Sizes: 14 Inch Tree. Comments: The Ornament Tree I had designed in 2001 was pastel when compared to this one. David's is very colorful, with lots of old fashioned glass ornaments.

## HEARTS (2003)

By: Diane Johnston. Introduced-2003. Retired-NA. Availability-Limited. Sizes: 6, 8, 11 Inch Plates; 9 Inch Bowl; 9, 11 Inch Fluted Bowls; 10 Inch Trays; 10 Inch Heart. Comments: This is our second Heart pattern. We retired the first one in 2001 and replaced it with Hearts and Roses. Customers seemed to want the more straightforward Hearts pattern, so Diane updated her 1994 version.

## RED, WHITE, & BLUE

By: David Switzer. Introduced-2003. Retired-NA. Availability-Average. Sizes: 8, 11, 14 Inch Plates; 9, 11, 14 Inch Bowls; 10 Inch Heart. Comments: After retiring Stars & Stripes in 2002, we decided we still wanted something patriotic in the line, so David came up with Red, White, & Blue.

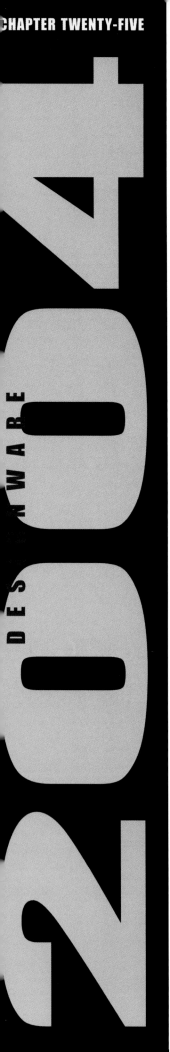

## CHAPTER TWENTY-FIVE

## ZINNIA (2004 COLLECTIBLE)

By: Peggy Karr. Introduced-2004. Retired-NA. Availability-Undetermined. Sizes: 11 Inch Plate. Comments: Zinnia is the fifth in the Limited Edition Collectable Series. The past four designs were a single color. In this plate I wanted to have multicolored flowers, so I chose the Zinnias for their wonderful salmon, orange, and yellow colors. Each is signed, dated, and numbered by me personally and comes with a certificate of authenticity. This plate was limited to production in the year 2004 only.

## BUTTERFLIES

By: Peggy Karr. Introduced-2004. Retired-NA. Availability-Undetermined. Sizes: 6, 8, 11, 14 Inch Plates; 9, 11 Inch Fluted Bowls; 10, 14 Inch Trays; 18 Inch Oval; 10 Inch Heart; 20 Inch Table. Comments: Meadow had been one of my favorite plates for a long time, so when we retired it I wanted to try my version of Butterflies. The ferns I used for the background had actually been designed by Diane for another plate that we didn't produce. I thought they would make the perfect background for this plate.

## HIBISCUS

By: Yolanda V. Fundora. Introduced-2004. Retired-NA. Availability-Undetermined. Sizes: 6, 8, 11, 14 Inch Plates; 10, 14 Inch Trays; 10 Inch Square; 20 Inch Table. Comments: We have a wonderful customer who has a chain of stores in Hawaii, so we try to keep a selection of tropical patterns in our catalog. Hibiscus makes me think of a warm tropical sunset with the sweet smell of flowers in the air.

## BIRDS

By: Yolanda V. Fundora. Introduced-2004. Retired-NA. Availability-Undetermined. Sizes: 8, 11, 14, 20 Inch Plates; 10, 14 Inch Trays; 10 Inch Square; 20 Inch Table. Comments: Birds have been a popular theme at Peggy Karr Glass. I have had one design, David has designed several, and now Yolanda has created her version of birds.

## WATER LILIES

By: David Switzer. Introduced-2004. Retired-NA. Availability-Undetermined. Sizes: 6, 8, 11, 14 Inch Plates; 9, 11 Inch Fluted Bowls; 10, 14 Inch Trays; 10 Inch Square. Comments: This is David's second Water Lily design. He did the first one in 1999, combining Koi and water lilies in the Koi Pond pattern.

*Art that has a Place in your Life...*

America's Premiere Fused Glass Design Studio

PEGGY KARR GLASS

## HYDRANGEA (2004)

By: Peggy Karr. Introduced-2004. Retired-NA. Availability-Undetermined. Sizes: 8, 11, 14 Inch Plates; 9, 11 Inch Bowls; 18 Inch Oval; 10 Inch Square. Comments: I had designed the first Hydrangea in 2000 for the Collectable Floral Series. I love the flowers and wanted to try putting them in a pot, much like the Geraniums which we designed in 2001.

## ANGEL

By: Yolanda V. Fundora. Introduced-2004. Retired-NA. Availability-Undetermined. Sizes: 6, 8, 11, 14 Inch Plates; 10, 14 Inch Trays; 10 Inch Square; 10 Inch Heart. Comments: Yolanda first designed the Angel for the tree shape only. Suzy had designed a successful Angel plate in 1994, which was retired in 1998. We had been trying to come up with another Angel but none of them quite measured up until this one.

## FRUITS

By: Peggy Karr. Introduced-2004. Retired-NA. Availability-Undetermined. Sizes: 8, 11, 14 Inch Plates; 9, 11, 14 Inch Bowls; 10, 14 Inch Trays; 10 Inch Square. Comments: A lot of people keep asking us to bring back the Checkerboard Fruit and Vegetable designs, so I gave it a try with a slightly different twist.

## JONQUILS

By: Yolanda V. Fundora. Introduced-2004. Retired-NA. Availability-Undetermined. Sizes: 8, 11, 14 Inch Plates; 9, 11 Inch Fluted Bowls; 10, 14 Inch Trays; 10 Inch Square; 10 Inch Heart. Comments: Jonquils was one of the first plates we did a little test market with. We set it up in our factory outlet store and asked people to vote on which version they liked the most. There were four variations with different colors and clear areas of glass. The one we eventually produced was the one with the most votes.

## CHANTICLEER

By: Diane Johnston. Introduced-2004. Retired-NA. Availability-Undetermined. Sizes: 8, 11, 14 Inch Plates; 9, 11 Inch Bowls; 10, 14 Inch Trays; 18 Inch Oval; 10 Inch Square. Comments: You often get a burning desire to change or update a plate after you have finished designing it because you have a lot of time to look at it after it's been put in the catalog and to consider what you would do differently. Diane created the first Rooster and just had to do another one.

## CHEFS

By: Yolanda V. Fundora. Introduced-2004. Retired-NA. Availability-Undetermined. Sizes: 8, 11 Inch Plates; 10, 14 Inch Trays; 18 Inch Oval; 10 Inch Square. Comments: We were trying to bring back some designs with our old checkerboard motif. When Yolanda came up with the Chefs, it seemed like the perfect place to add the checkerboard.

## MARTINI

By: Yolanda V. Fundora. Introduced-2004. Retired-NA. Availability-Undetermined. Sizes: 8, 11 Inch Plates; 9 Inch Bowl; 10 Inch Tray; 10 Inch Square. Comments: Martini was a last minute addition in 2004. We originally thought it was too contemporary for the catalog, but when customers saw a sample they loved it, so we added it to the line.

## BIRTHDAY

By: Billy Brisley. Introduced-2004. Retired-NA. Availability-Undetermined. Sizes: 6, 8, 11, 14 Inch Plates. Comments: We were all skeptical of Billy's idea for Birthday, but when it was finished we fell in love with it. It's just one of those designs that puts a smile on your face and helps make birthdays special.

## PINEAPPLE (2004)

By: Diane Johnston & Yolanda V. Fundora. Introduced-2004. Retired-NA. Availability-Undetermined. Sizes: 8, 11, 14 Inch Plates; 10, 14 Inch Trays; 10 Inch Square. Comments: Pineapple was the third plate designed in the "Bombay" style. Diane had done the first two and we thought that Yolanda's Pineapple from 2000 would be prefect for the third plate in the group.

## ORCHID

By: Diane Johnston. Introduced-2004. Retired-NA. Availability-Undetermined. Sizes: 8, 11, 14 Inch Plates; 10, 14 Inch Trays; 10 Inch Square. Comments: Orchid was the first plate Diane designed in the "Bombay" style. We liked it so much we added the Palm and the Pineapple to create a series.

## PALM

By: Diane Johnston. Introduced-2004. Retired-NA. Availability-Undetermined. Sizes: 8, 11, 14 Inch Plates; 10, 14 Inch Trays; 10 Inch Square. Comments: Palm was the second plate designed in the "'Bombay" style. We kept seeing Palm Trees on everything so after Diane did Orchid we decided to use the same background and add a Palm Tree.

## CACTUS (2004)

By: Peggy Karr. Introduced-2004. Retired-NA. Availability-Undetermined. Sizes: 8, 11, 14 Inch Plates; 10 Inch Tray; 10 Inch Square; 20 Inch Table. Comments: Our Southwest Reps kept asking for a new design for their territory. I saw a beautiful photograph of an old pueblo Indian pot with a cactus and it gave me the inspiration for this design.

## WHITE POINTSETTIA

By: David Switzer. Introduced-2004. Retired-NA. Availability-Undetermined. Sizes: 6, 8, 11, 14, 20 Inch Plates; 9, 11 Inch Bowls; 10, 14 Inch Trays; 18 Inch Oval; 10 Inch Square; 10 Inch Heart; 20 Inch Table. Comments: I think this plate is absolutely fabulous. It started out with a different flower in the center, but when David changed it to a white Poinsettia it just made the plate perfect. The details in the border give it a rich, traditional look.

## TEDDY BEAR TREE

By: Diane Johnston. Introduced-2004. Retired-NA. Availability-Undetermined. Sizes: 14 Inch Tree. Comments: We had such success with the other tree shapes that a teddy bear was a natural fit. Diane did a great job creating a cute teddy bear that everyone loved.

*Art that has a Place in your Life...*

America's Premiere Fused Glass Design Studio

PEGGY KARR GLASS

## ANGEL TREE

By: Yolanda V. Fundora. Introduced-2004. Retired-NA.
Availability-Undetermined. Sizes: 14 Inch Tree. Comments:
Angel tree was designed first. We thought it was cute, so
we created an entire line with this angel.

## HALLOWEEN (2004)

By: Peggy Karr. Introduced-2004. Retired-NA. Availability-Undetermined. Sizes: 6, 8, 11, 14 Inch Plates; 9, 11,
14 Inch Bowls; 10, 14 Inch Trays; 10 Inch Square.
Comments: Halloween has always been one of my
favorite holidays. I had spent a lot of time designing cats
for the Widow Cat plate which I did the year before so I
had a lot of good reference to work with. I had seen a
Crow on top of a pumpkin someplace and thought it
was just what the design needed to bring it to life.

## SCHOOL DAYS

By: Billy Brisley. Introduced-2004. Retired-NA. Availability-Undetermined. Sizes: 6, 8, 11 Inch Plates; 10 Inch Tray. Comments: School
Days started out as an ornament Billy created for teacher's gifts at the
end of the year. It looked so cute we felt it would do well as a set of
small pieces for others to give their teachers.

## CHAPTER TWENTY-SIX

When Colorware was first introduced in 1994 we were all very excited. I thought glass dinnerware was going to be the next big thing. Colorware was first available in six different patterns, twenty-one color choices, and twelve various sizes of bowls and plates. If you do the math, it comes to 1512 possible choices. It hadn't occurred to us what that meant until we tried to make and sell it. The stores had a difficult time trying to figure out which plates to buy and it wasn't easy for us to figure out how to make them. Trying to keep an inventory of all those plates was just as hard as trying to make them to order. We usually made a few more plates than needed for an order in case some of them were rejected in quality control. That saved us the time waiting for the rejected plates to be remade. On the other hand, it always left a few extra plates we didn't need. Well, they added up very quickly and even if they were sold we had to find them in the endless piles. We figured it out

Original cover shot for Colorware catalog. Table setting of Harvest Fruit with Rattan Colorware in Golden and Green. 1994.

pretty quickly and in 1995 Colorware was cut down to only two patterns, the colors to eleven, and the shapes to ten. That left us with 220 possibilities, which was much easier to manage but still left the stores a little confused. In 1997 Colorware was retired for lack of sales. Our prices were too high for casual dinnerware, but it was the best we could do given the hand-made process. When the collection of odds and ends was sold at our Second Sale people loved picking through and creating mix and match sets. I still think they were a great idea. Today glass dinnerware is becoming more and more popular; maybe we were just a little ahead of the times. Who knows, it may be time to try it again.

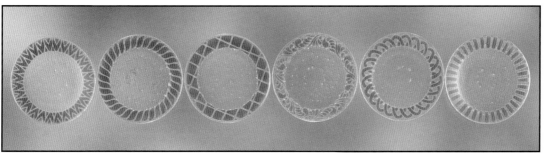

Original 6 patterns. Left-right: Tribal, Classic, Parquet, Filigree, Rattan, and Eclipse.

COLORWARE

Original sizes. Left, top to bottom: 20", 16", 14", 11", 10", 8", 6" plates. Right, top to bottom: 8", 10", 11", 14", 16" bowls.

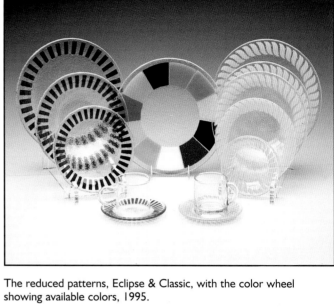

The reduced patterns, Eclipse & Classic, with the color wheel showing available colors, 1995.

Original colors.

### Colors:

| | | |
|---|---|---|
| Black 01 | Red 02 | White 03 |
| Salmon 04 | Peach 05 | Pumpkin 06 |
| Golden 07 | Caramel 08 | Marigold 09 |
| Green 10 | Avocado 11 | Mint 12 |
| Peacock 13 | Seafoam 14 | Aqua 15 |
| Cobalt 16 | Royal 17 | Cadet 18 |
| Blackberry 19 | Pansy 20 | Pink 21 |

Table setting mixing Colorware with Sun & Moon.

Table setting mixing Black and Gold Eclipse Colorware.

Montage of Colorware and Designware.

## CHAPTER TWENTY-SEVEN

Clocks were introduced in 1992. I first got the idea after sharing a Show Room in Atlanta with Santa Barbara Ceramic Design. They made these wonderful clocks out of highly decorated ceramic tiles. We started by simply adding numbers to our eight and eleven-inch plate designs and firing them flat. They were ok but one was too big and the other too small, so in 1994 we settled on our nine-inch bowl size. In the beginning they sold very well and over the years we made a total of sixty-one different clocks before they were retired in 2000.

We came up with some new innovations to help produce the clocks. When the bowls were first designed they worked perfectly well, but when the design was fired flat to make the clocks there were lots of big bubbles. Part of the reason was the numbers enameled around the outside edge. To solve the problem, I developed special ink we could use to silkscreen the numbers onto the glass. The ink was smooth and perfect, which made the numbers easier to read and reduced the bubbles. We went on to use the silkscreen ink in some of our later designs to add black-line details.

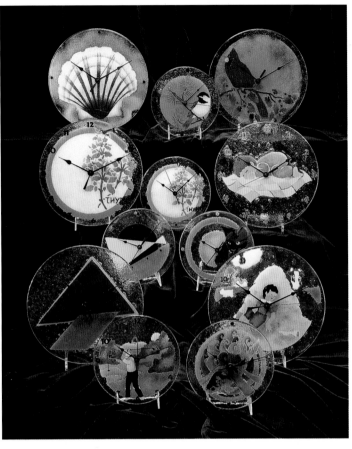

Original photograph of first clocks showing 11" and 8" sizes, 1992.

We designed the clocks to hang on the wall, but you could also put them on a plate stand to display them on a shelf. This was often lost on the stores, who would say they didn't have enough wall space to display them. Another problem was although the plates looked great, as a clock they were a little busy. All the detail made the clock hard to read from a distance. That, coupled with the hands getting bent and causing the clock to stop working, forced us to retire them in 2000. During the course of writing this book I have looked at some of our retired items and thought they were a good idea that just needed a little more tweaking. After looking at the clocks again, I think I could solve the problems today.

SPECIAL NOTE: since most of our clocks came from our Designware patterns, I have only included a sampling here. If the pattern came in a clock, it is listed in the description with the design photograph.

**Nine inch Clocks:**
Veggie
Fruit
Harvest Fruit
Harvest Vegetable

Cat
Cow
Pig
Harvest Grape

Hunt
Dogwood
Hummingbird
Herb

Summer Garden
Spring Garden
Victorian Wreath
Sunflower

Columns
Metropolis
Sun
Stars

Ivy
Marsh
Raccoon
Frogs

**Nine inch Clocks:**
Hearts
Rabbit
Carousel
Kittens

Boating
Scallop
Seashells
Tropical Fish

Skier
Golf Green
Cardinal
Chickadee

Geo Yellow
Geo Cobalt
Renaissance Bright
Mammy

Humpty
Boy Blue
Little Bo Peep
Baby

Baseball
Football
Soccer
Basketball

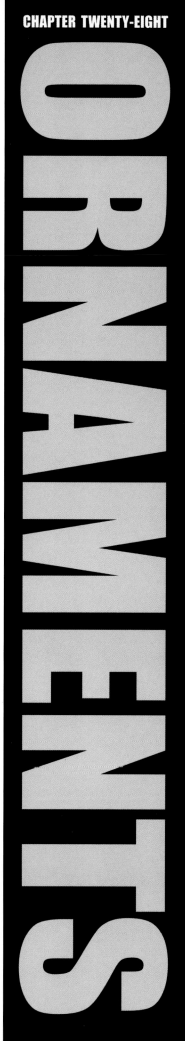

## CHAPTER TWENTY-EIGHT

# ORNAMENTS

Ornaments have been a fabulous addition to Peggy Karr Glass. They are made from a three-inch round single layer of glass with the enamels on the surface. A hole is drilled before they are decorated and fired so we can attach a ribbon for hanging. We have found many uses for them over the years. They can be used as suncatchers; napkin rings; decorations for gift packages; the list goes on. Ornaments were first introduced in 1993 and are still made today. We have made over three hundred different ornaments since the beginning, but our most famous ornaments were the ones produced for L.L. Bean in 1994. Twenty-four thou-

First Ornament Box, 1992. It required a lot of time to assemble so we later changed to a jewelry box with a clear lid.

sand rabbits, moose, loons, and bears were produced and we never wanted to see another one by the time we were finished. It was a wonderful learning experience and taught us how to plan and produce large volumes of work. We began by enameling four ornaments at a time and then figured out how to do six, which made the task go faster and more efficiently.

When the ornaments first came out we used a colored ribbon with a little bow to hang them. I designed a jig to hold the ornaments so you could hand tie the bows evenly every time. We had an employee named Diane who would sit and happily tie the bows all day long. We kept producing more and more ornaments to the point that even Diane said enough is enough! We found a company that would make the ribbon into a closed circle so all we had to do was loop it through the ornament. NO MORE BOWS!!! Another great story concerns the little boxes they came in. The first one required a lot of assembly. It had a window opening front and back so you could see the ornament inside. You had to carefully punch out the windows before you folded each box. It was a time consuming task. EVERYONE sat and folded boxes. We took them home, we folded them at lunch, and I think I used to fold them in my sleep. We finally decided this was crazy and found a small jewelry box with a clear lid, which is what we still use today.

We usually have between sixty and eighty ornaments available for sale at any given time, so we are constantly retiring and adding new ones to the line. All the ornaments with an "*" are currently (2004) available. It is interesting to see that we have some very old ornaments still in the line today.

The first actual ornaments were the Songbirds designed by David Switzer in 1992. Our first major introduction came in 1993 and those ornaments are pictured in their entirety.

**\*Indicates ornaments currently available 2004**

**Left to right:**
Cherry
Pear
Grape
Peach
Apple
Lemon

Tomato
Eggplant
Chili
Bean
Carrot
Corn

Marsh Marigold
Star Flower
Jack-in-Pulpit
Bee Balm
Calypso Lily
Columbine

Cow
Dog
Pig
Cat
Rooster
Ram

Trout Lily
Lady Slipper
Trillium
Bluets
Turks Cap Lily
Squirrel Corn

Goose
Horse
Rabbit
Buffalo
Lobster
Scotty

*Cardinal
Chickadee
Bluebird
Goldfinch
*Hummingbird
Scarlet Tanager

Chives
Thyme
Dill
Rosemary
Mint
Sage

Painted Bunting
Blackbird
Robin
Meadowlark
Oriole
Cedar Waxwing

Football
Baseball
Basketball
*Golf
Tennis
Soccer

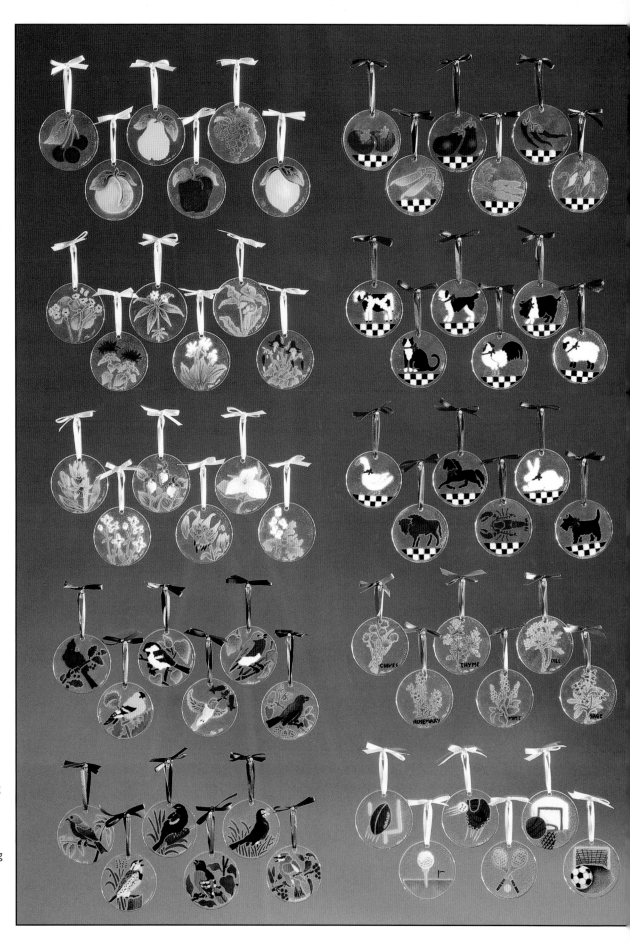

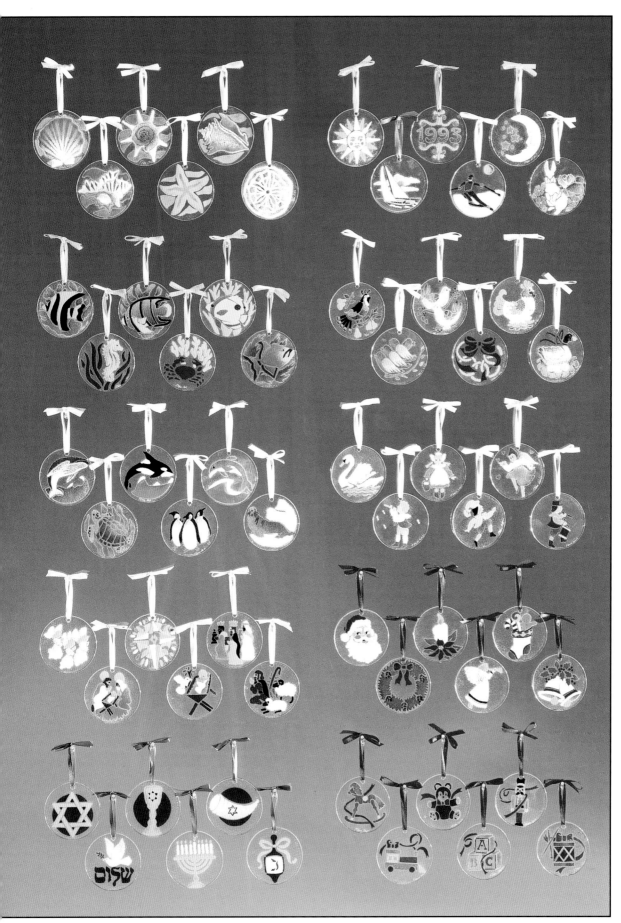

**Left to right:**

Scallop
Triumph Star
Conch
Whelk
Starfish
Sand Dollar

Sun
Limited Edition
Moon
Boating
Skier
Rabbit

Moorish Idol
Queen Angel
Butterfly Fish
Sea Horse
Crab
Triggerfish

Partridge
Turtle Doves
French Hens
Colly Birds
Golden Rings
Geese

Humpback
Orca
*Dolphin
Sea Turtle
Penguins
Seal

Swans
Maids
Ladies
Pipers
Lords
Drummers

Angels
Star
Wise men
Mary & Joseph
Crèche
Shepherd

*Santa
Candle
Stocking
Pine Wreath
Trumpeting Angel
Bells

Star of David
Kiddush Cup
Shofar
Shalom & Dove
Menorah
Dreidel

Rocking Horse
Bear
Nutcracker
Train
Blocks
Drum

Moon, Sun, Stars, *Rabbit, Carousel, Limited Edition, 1994.

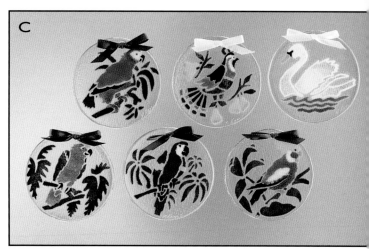

A. Corn Flower, Daffodil, Primrose, Zinnia, Pansy, Daisy, 1994.
B. Poppy, Iris, Lily, Rose, Peony, Tulip, 1994.
C. African Grey, Partridge, Swan, Amazon, Macaw, Cockatiel, 1994.

A. Cross & Crown, Hands all Around, Starry Sky, Rising Sun, Bear Claw, Blazing Star, 1994.
B. Baby, Coffee, Tea, Boating, Skiing, Lighthouse, 1994.

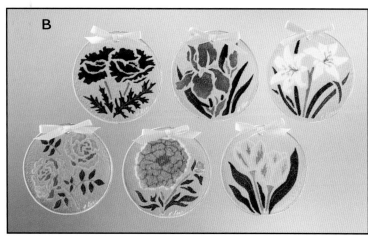

A. *Purple Pansy, Red Pansy, Yellow Pansy, Lilac, Magnolia, Bluebonnet, 1994.
B. Valentine, *Wedding, *Hearts, Piano, French Horn, Violin, 1994.

A. Pumpkins, Moon, Witch, Cat, Ghost, Owl, 1996.
B. Stars, 1996, Ornament, Tree, *St. Nick, *Snowman, 1996.

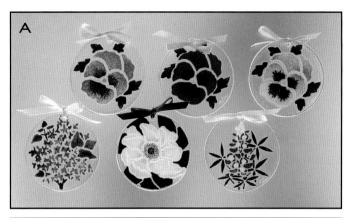

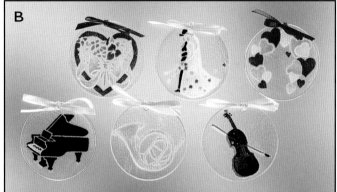

Bunny-Cart, Rabbit, Carousel, Bunny-Basket, Bunny-Brush, Bunny-Carrot, 1996.

Party Mask, Music, Theater Masks, Top Hat, Noise Makers, 1996.

*Monarch, *Swallowtail, Spotted Burnet, Rose,
Red Stripe, Blue Surgeon, Yellow Tang, 1996.

Ornaments pictured below were introduced between
1998 and 1999.

*Chilies.

Ducks.

Rooster.

Teddy Bear, 1999.

Yachting.

Horse.

Sunflower.

Circle of Hope.

Cross.

Holly Wreath.

*Snowflake.

2000 Globe.

Church.

Holly Tree.

Globe.

2000.

Ornaments pictured below were introduced in 2000.

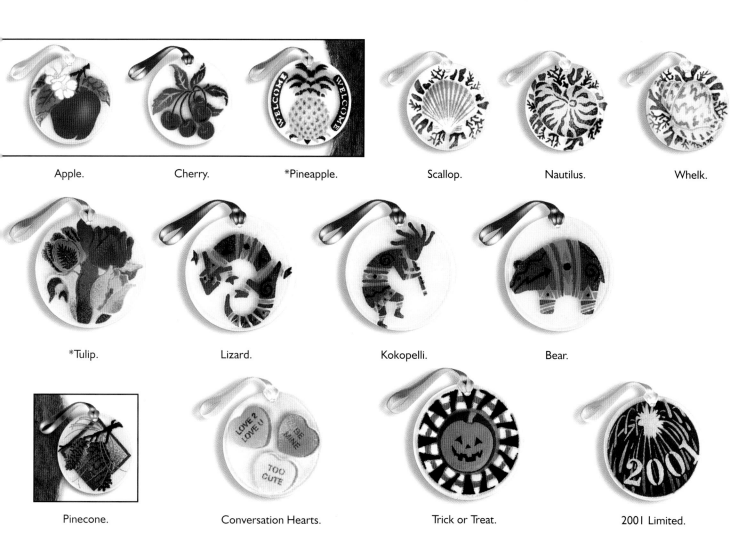

Apple.     Cherry.     *Pineapple.     Scallop.     Nautilus.     Whelk.

*Tulip.     Lizard.     Kokopelli.     Bear.

Pinecone.     Conversation Hearts.     Trick or Treat.     2001 Limited.

The next group of ornaments pictured were introduced in 2001.

Eggs.     *Daffodil.     *Flamingo.     *Heralding Angel.

Stork.     Topiary.     *Father Christmas.     *Wreath.

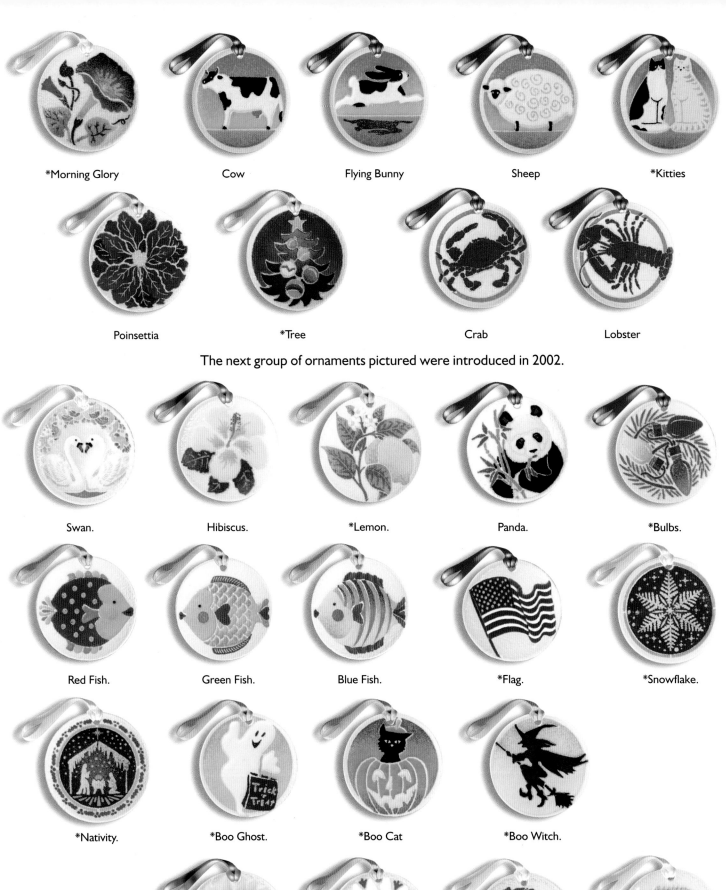

*Morning Glory

Cow

Flying Bunny

Sheep

*Kitties

Poinsettia

*Tree

Crab

Lobster

The next group of ornaments pictured were introduced in 2002.

Swan.

Hibiscus.

*Lemon.

Panda.

*Bulbs.

Red Fish.

Green Fish.

Blue Fish.

*Flag.

*Snowflake.

*Nativity.

*Boo Ghost.

*Boo Cat

*Boo Witch.

Ornaments pictured
were introduced in 2003.

*Sunflower.

*Daisy.

*Rose.

*Yellow Tropical Fish.

*Red Stripe Fish.      *Tees.      *Rooftop Santa.      *Candy Canes.      *Cat.

*Moose.      *Cookies.

The next group
of ornaments were
introduced in 2004.

*Hibiscus.      *Goldfinch.

*Dice.      Cards.      *Hydrangea.      *Chanticleer.      *Grapes.

*Chef.      *Happy Birthday.      *School Days.      *Teddy Bear.      *White Poinsettia.

The final group of ornaments pictured are our Collectables Series. We introduced them in
2001 and we come out with three new examples each year with the same background colors.

Collectables 2001: Santa, Deer, Home.

Collectables 2003: Gingerbread, Bells, Snowman.

Collectables 2002: Santa, Tree, Flake.

Collectables 2004: *Cardinal, *Pinecone, *Stocking.

## CHAPTER TWENTY-NINE

# ROUNDELS

Ad shot showing the three original sizes of Roundels. Christmas Day 11 inch; St. Nick 8 inch; and Sleigh 6 inch.

Roundels were added in 1994. They came in three sizes: 6, 8, and 11 inches. I had made a lot of sun-catchers in my stained glass days, so I thought these would be a big hit. Basically they were just a larger version of our ornaments that people already used as "little" sun-catchers. They came with a chain for hanging but they never caught on like the ornaments. We only made about fifty different designs. They were made from our 6, 8, and 11 inch plate patterns and fired flat without the top piece of glass. If you look at the captions in the plate designs it will tell you if the pattern came in a Roundel. They were retired in 1999. Below are some examples of 6 and 8 inch Roundels.

Six inch Roundels, left to right: Yachting, Shalom, Rooster, Daisy, Iris, Golf Course, Garden Cat, Pansy, Sun, Chili, Coral Reef, Halloween, St. Nick, Spring Garden, Snowman, Hummingbird & Hibiscus, Bouquet.

Eight inch Roundels, left to right: Angels, St. Nick, Poinsettia, Christmas Day, Winter Wreath, Stars, Star of David, Shalom, Cornucopia, Halloween, Easter Basket.

Eight inch Roundels, left to right: Spring Garden, Garden Cat, Sun, Iris, Cow, Pansy, Magnolia, Cherubs, Lilac, Harvest Fruit, Hummingbird & Hibiscus.

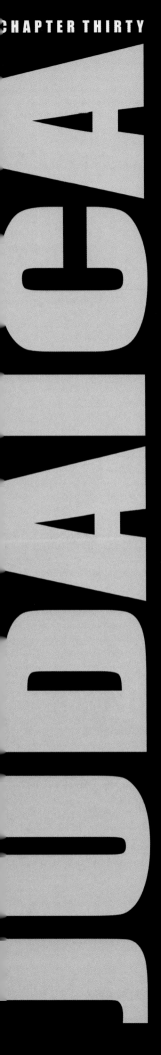

## CHAPTER THIRTY

I can't remember if I came up with the first Seder Plate idea or someone asked me to make one. Either way, I first designed them in 1989. It was very difficult to make the molds needed to fire them as there were six round depressions running around the rim of the 14 inch plate to place the different remembrances used during the Seder Dinner at Passover. I made all the molds by hand and had to be careful that all the depressions were the same depth, otherwise the plates wouldn't sit flat and they would wobble on the table. When we first introduced them everyone loved them. They were a fresh new approach to a mostly very traditional plate. The first Seder plates had symbols and the later ones had both Hebrew and English words to indicate what went in the round depressions. We used the silkscreen technique to help reduce the bubbles in the words in 1994.

As time passed we added more to the line. We started with 11 inch round Matzo and then went to the square 10 inch plate.

Chanukah 14 inch tray by Donna Orsini, 1999.

We also did a 14 inch round Shalom and Shabbat and later a 18 inch oval Shabbat plate. All had matching borders to the Seder plates. Lastly, we added a 14 inch rectangular Chanukah plate and Special Wedding Plates to the line. There were nineteen different Seder plates, which were the most popular, followed by the Wedding Plates that had the Hebrew maxim, "I am my beloved's and my beloved is mine". We retired the Judaic line in 2002.

Early Seder plates, 1989: *Leaf, *Swirl, Grape. (*Choice of color.)

Early Seder plates, 1989: Floral, *Geometric, *Solid Band. (*Choice of color.)

Early Checkerboard Shabbat, Matzo, Seder, 1989. (Choice of checkerboard color.)

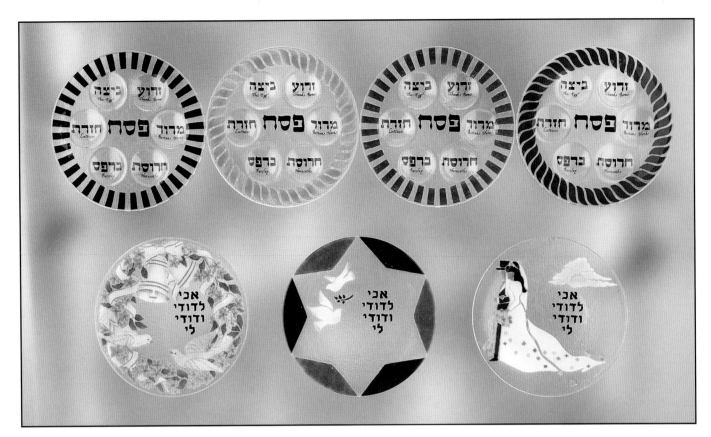

Later Judaic, 1994: Colorware Seder plates available in various colors, Hebrew Bells, Star of David Wedding, Hebrew Wedding.

Hebrew Bride & Groom, 1998.

Checkerboard Seder & Matzo

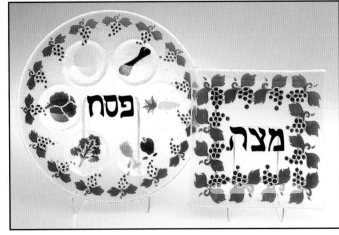

Grape Seder & Matzo.

Multi-Star Seder & Matzo.

Star of David Seder & Matzo.

Gold Eclipse Seder & Matzo.

Tribal Seder & Matzo.

Seder, Matzo & Shabbat in Morning Glory, Persian Blues, Harvest Grape, and Pansy.

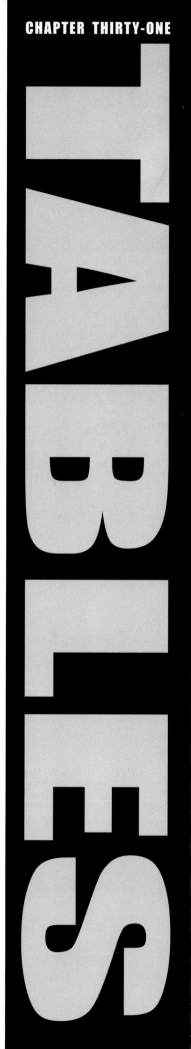

## CHAPTER THIRTY-ONE

We first started making tables in 1992. I am not sure how I came up with the idea for the first table but I think it came when we decided to add The Highpoint Furniture Market to our list of wholesale shows. As it's name implies, it is the largest wholesale furniture and decorative accessory show in North America. It is held in Highpoint, North Carolina, takes over the entire town, and goes on for nine days. I created the tables hoping their uniqueness would draw attention to our booth. The show was huge and covered many buildings; our location was not the best and neither were our sales. We learned that Highpoint just wasn't our market, but we did get a lot of good feedback and people really liked our new tables.

The first two metal bases were very simple. One had four straight legs with a cross in the middle to hold it together while the other was a tripod with bent legs that were welded together in the center. I designed them and we had a local metal fabricator cut all the iron and bend the legs for the tripod. We assembled and painted them ourselves. The company we used to cut and bend the metal moved away so we decided to buy a small bender and band saw so we could do all the work ourselves. It gave us a lot more flexibility to try new ideas, plus we didn't have to wait for the metal guy to get around to filling our order, which could sometimes take forever if he was in the middle of a big job.

In the beginning we were able to produce all our own table bases, but as time passed it got harder and harder to keep up with the demand. We just weren't set up to do all that metal work on our little band saw and bender. We eventually found someone who would do all the work for us at a price we could afford. Our ability to fabricate the tables was limited but the new manufacturer was very talented and it wasn't long before we started to add new designs with a lot more pizzazz. All our tables are 21 inches tall and our glass tops are either 20 inches round or 16 inches square. They are all made with four layers of glass that added up to about a 1/2 inch thickness for the tabletop. Almost all of our 20 inch platters could be had as a table and are listed in the description for each of our patterns in the Designware section of this book. We currently produce about twenty-five different glass tops and six different bases. We just added a brand new height of 29 inches this year.

Ad shot for early 4-leg table base with Checker Board Game Top surrounded by stars. 1992.

Early Basic 4-leg & 3-leg bases introduced in 1992 with 20" round tops: Coral Reef, Pansy, and Daisy.

Early Basic 4-leg & 3-leg bases introduced in 1992 with 16" square tops: Chilies, Checkers with Stars, and Rooster.

Ad shot for Basic 4-leg base with Antique Floral 20" glass top, 1995.

Ad shot for Spiral 4-leg base added 1999 with Gardening 20" glass top, 1999.

Spiral Pedestal added 1999 with Birds 20" glass top, 2004.

Ringed 4-leg base added 2002 with Golf Tees 20" glass top, 2003.

Multi-Twist 4-leg base added 2002 with Butterfly 20" glass top, 2004.

Wine on Multi-Twist 4-leg base added in 2002.

20" Folding 4-leg base added in 2004 with Cactus 20" glass top, 2004.

29" Folding 4-leg base added in 2004 with Poinsettia 20" glass top, 2004.

Ad shot for new Palm Tree table top on Multi-Twist 4-leg base, 2004.

First ad shot for our new metal plate stands: Gong Stand, Bowl Stand, Wall Stand, and Chip & Dip. 1998.

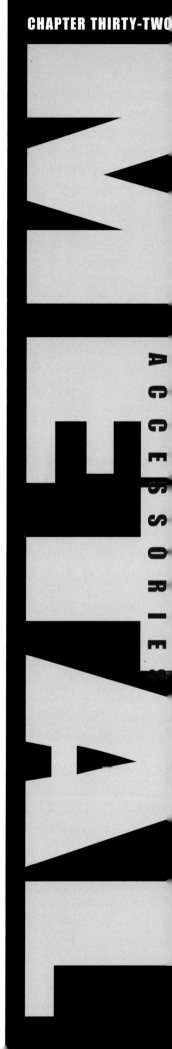

## CHAPTER THIRTY-TWO

We introduced Metal accessories in 1998 and they have been a wonderful addition to our line. They can be used to display the plates for decoration or make them functional for serving. A small company we found at a Trade Show made our first metal accessories. They were located in Florida and everything went smoothly for a while. As our sales increased, it became harder and harder for them to keep up with our demand. In 2000, we had to turn to a larger manufacturer. Since then we have found a new company that is very creative and able to design more elegant stands. They provide us with great quality. We are looking forward to coming out with some really interesting new designs.

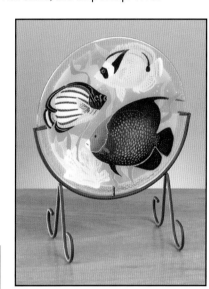

Under the Sea with gong stand, introduced 1998.

Daisies with bowl stand, introduced 1998.

Rooftop Santa with wall stand, introduced 1998.

Chilies with "Chip and Dip" stand, introduced 1998.

Tuscany with 10" two-tier square/rectangle stand, introduced 2003.

Ornaments tree with easel stand, introduced 2001.

White Poinsettia with 14" rectangle serving stand, introduced 2004.

Wine with "All Occasion Lamp," introduced 2002. The lamp was designed to hold any of our 11 inch plates and can be changed to fit any occasion.

Chef's with 18" oval serving stand, introduced 2004.

## CHAPTER THIRTY-THREE

In 1997 we started to make promotional materials for our retailers. They wanted printed postcards they could use for mailings to their customers. We print them in very large quantities, which makes them much less expensive. We make these postcards available to our stores at our cost. Another type of promotional item we make for our customers is our Consumer Brochure. It is a condensed version of our regular wholesale catalog, which has pictures of all our current patterns.

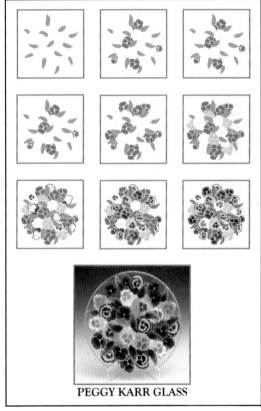

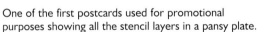

One of the first postcards used for promotional purposes showing all the stencil layers in a pansy plate.

Another early postcard showing the 20" and an 11" Veggie plates.

1998 Postcard showing the Chilies, Gardening, Tropical Floral, Pansies, and Coral Reef patterns.

1998 Care-tag cover showing Pansies, Coral Reef, and Snowman.

*Everyday Treasures*

By Peggy Karr Glass **2001**

Cover of 2001 Consumer Brochure. This is the first one ever produced. It gave a complete listing of the year's line.

*Left:*
2000 Postcard showing the Partridge in a Pear Tree, Holly, Snowman, Sleigh, St. Nick, and Ornaments patterns.

*Below:*
Inside of 1998 Care-tag showing Rooster, Tropical Floral, Autumn Sunflowers, Halloween, a Chilies chip-and-dip set, and a Gardening Tabletop.

Welcome to the unique world of **Peggy Karr Glass**. Established in 1987, Peggy Karr Glass is the premier American design studio of handmade, fused glass giftware. Peggy Karr Glass is suitable for every occasion. Designs are available in a wide variety of sizes and shapes, and we offer an extensive collection of accessories to complement our glass products.

The designs pictured here and many more can be found or ordered at the fine business named on the back of this card. If no name appears or the retailer is inconveniently located, visit our web site at www.PEGGYKARRGLASS.com or call 1-800-754-8585 for assistance.

2001 Christmas Treasures Postcard showing Father Christmas, Tree, Ornaments, St. Nick, Partridge in a Pear Tree, Holly, and Snowman patterns.

2001 Everyday Treasures Postcard showing Morning Glories, Seafood, Orchard, Gourmet Garden, Daffodils, Tulips, Persian Blues, and Geraniums patterns.

2002 Postcard showing Geraniums, Haunted House, Snowguy, Fish Frolics Blue Fish, Wine, Animal Frolics Kitties, Lemons, Morning Glory.

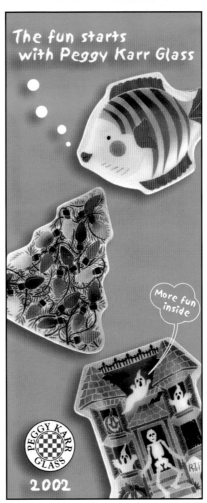

Cover of 2002 Consumer Brochure.

Cover of 2003 Consumer Brochure showing Tuscany.

Cover of 2004 Consumer Brochure showing the 11" Butterflies plate.

2003 Postcard showing part of the Tuscany line.

2004 Postcard showing Chefs, Hydrangea, White Poinsettia, and Butterflies.

2004 Care-tag cover showing Teddy Tree, Chef, and Tuscany plates.

2004 Care-tag interior spread showing Chanticleer, Chilies, Wine, Hydrangea, Palm, White Poinsettia, and Birds.